ACCIDENTAL

Times

ACCIDENTAL

Times

a selection of bizarre and amusing
Victorian accidents from

The Times

compiled by
Jane Lambert

illustrated by
Bill Tidy

London
GEORGE ALLEN & UNWIN
Boston   Sydney

**George Allen & Unwin (Publishers) Ltd,
40 Museum Street, London WC1A 1LU**

8271

This edition and selection © Jane Lambert 1984
Illustrations © Bill Tidy 1984

43222

British Library Cataloguing in Publication Data

Lambert, Jane
  Accidental Times.
1. Accidents
I. Title
363.1   HV675
ISBN 0–04–808041–1

Set in 11 on 12 point Plantin by
Nene Phototypesetters Ltd, Northampton
and printed in Great Britain by
Richard Clay (The Chaucer Press) Ltd,
Bungay, Suffolk

Contents

To Stephen, who makes everything possible

Acknowledgements

I should like to acknowledge the patient assistance given me by the staff of the Cambridge University Microfilm Reading Room, especially by Pat Lewis, hoping it will make her smile.

Introduction

This book is the result of several months' hard labour in a dark, airless microfilm reading-room in the University Library at Cambridge. It was conceived while I was doing research on other topics which required me to consult Palmer's Index to *The Times*. While thus engaged I frequently found myself distracted by entries under the heading of 'Accidents'. During the middle of the last century someone at *The Times* seems to have been on the look-out for bizarre and mysterious happenings. It was impossible to resist inquiring further into descriptions such as: 'Accident to M. Dumas, from Swallowing a Glass of Nitric Acid Poured out by his Monkey in Sport', or 'to Eliz. Kenchen, Strangled by her own Bonnet-Strings'. I have selected around 140 of these curiosities to share with you, and Bill Tidy has added some wonderfully witty illustrations for your further amusement.

The accidents offer a fascinating insight into the lives of the Victorians. Theirs seems to have been a world infinitely more hazardous than our own: poisons were freely available, guns were universally owned, gunpowder was used to clean kitchen stoves, horses were continually running off with their carriages and, at the theatre, the footlights were still naked flames. And yet, paradoxically, the Victorians seem to have been more reckless, more carefree, more enterprising. You will meet people who carry nitric acid in their pockets, drink unknown substances with dire effects, shoot themselves with their own guns and go bathing when they can't swim. You will find the bizarre and the poignant, absurd feats, miraculous escapes and monumental bad luck stories.

Many of the accidents were reprinted from other journals, but there is uniformly a delight in prurient detail: I have seen several angry letters in subsequent issues which attempt to put the record straight – too late, of course. It all testifies to the strange mixture of the sensational and the coy which characterizes the Victorian outlook. There is also a keen sense of the ridiculous, and for some reprehensible unfortunates *The Times* even reserves a censorious, 'serves-you-right' tone.

I have taken three liberties. The first is in using the term 'Victorian' to describe the accidents, when, as you will see, a few of them fall outside the period. I have also used the word 'accident' in its fullest sense, so that I could include mishaps and calamities not strictly 'accidents'. Finally, I have preserved the wonderful idiosyncracies of spelling, punctuation and expression wherever possible, rather than adopting a more modern, punctilious approach.

I hope you will enjoy reading this book as much as I enjoyed compiling it!

The bizarre . . .

ASSAULT BY MADMAN

On Saturday evening, about six o'clock, a gentleman called in great haste at the station-house, Marylebone-lane, and stated that a madman, residing in the second floor of the house of Mr. Willis, music-seller, Lower Grosvenor-street, had nearly killed his medical attendant. Two constables were immediately dispatched to the spot, and on their arrival ascertained that the name of the deranged person, who is a gentleman of property, was Broadly, and the injured party Mr. Vance, surgeon, of Sackville-street, Piccadilly. A keeper had been provided by the friends of Mr. Broadly to watch him, but his madness not being of a violent nature, no personal restraint was thought necessary. That afternoon Mr. Vance, as usual, called to see his patient, who, on his reaching the second-floor landing, came out of his room to meet him, and putting out his hand said, "How do you do, doctor?" Without giving him time to reply, Mr. Broadly lifted him off his feet and hurled him head foremost over the bannisters, and then pushed his keeper into the room, and following himself barricaded the door. The constables burst open the door, when, after a desperate struggle, they succeeded in securing the madman, who continually vociferated "Oh, Marie Taglioni!" He was conveyed to a private mad-house at Kensington. Mr. Vance was taken to his residence, where, on examination, it was discovered that, besides being otherwise seriously injured, his skull was severely fractured, and he now lies in a very precarious state.

28 March 1837

1

THE DECOY WORKED BUT
SERGEANT GROYNES
DRESS IS RUINED!

STRANGE BEHAVIOUR IN THE STRAND

A correspondent, who gives his name and address, has sent the following statement:— Two ladies were yesterday afternoon walking together in the Strand, and an elderly man, of short stature, with a bundle under his arm, in appearance much like a Spitalfields weaver, followed close behind them, for a short distance, and from his mouth squirted over the silk dresses of both ladies an acid liquid that entirely destroyed the colours of both their silk dresses. Within these few days many ladies' dresses have, we are told, been entirely spoilt in the same manner.

5 December 1829

SINGULAR RUN

As the Regulator coach from Falmouth to Exeter, about a fortnight since, was changing horses at Crockernwell, whilst the horse-keeper was engaged in taking out those which had gone the stage from Okehampton, owing to some sudden impulse, the fresh horses, which had been led out, and were standing ready tackled, with their cloths on, suddenly started off without the coach, running the whole way to Exeter, about 11 miles. What is very singular, the animals kept together the entire distance, as if they had been yoked to the coach, under a coachman's guidance. On their arrival at the Exeter gate the turnpike man stared not a little, as did many others on the road, to see the horses without their burden, and surmising some accident, of course took charge of them. The horse-keeper, in his fright, followed, but was soon distanced, arriving, however, only half an hour after the horses. It is remarkable that the horses kept their accustomed time, and that only one of them lost its cloth on the way. The coach went on with the other horses. *(West Briton)*

13 April 1841

WONDERFUL TOAD

The 'Journal de l'Aveyron' relates that a woman aged about 60, while at work in the fields at Saint Come, had her foot seized by an enormous toad, which held so fast that it could not be forced to let go until it was pierced through by a man with a sharp pointed stick. Only a few drops of blood followed the bite, and the woman continued her work, but in a very short time her countenance became flushed, and she experienced a burning thirst, but went to bed without taking any remedies. In the morning she was found dead, and the autopsy of the body gave all the symptoms of death from the poison of a venomous reptile, thus contradicting the opinion of naturalists that toads do not possess any venomous qualities.

17 June 1841

WONDERFUL

The 'Journal de Nevers' contains the following incredible statement:— "A young man, 27 years of age, who was playing with some companions, fell to the ground, having at the time an open table-knife in his mouth. In the fall he swallowed the knife, and was for some time seriously ill, with repeated vomiting. At length he recovered, although the knife had never been discharged, and he had almost forgotten the accident. Latterly, 20 months after the event, a swelling, attended with violent inflammation, took place in his side, and an abscess was formed, which was in due time opened by the surgeons. A few days afterwards the point of the knife made its appearance, and at length the whole knife was drawn out. When it was swallowed it was six inches in length, but during its stay in his body the handle and the blade had both been reduced, so that the knife measured only four inches and a half. The young man is now perfectly well."
(Galignani's Messenger)

12 November 1842

BITE FROM A CENTIPEDE

Yesterday morning a dock labourer, named Joseph Fox, while engaged on board the Caroline, in the West India Dock, which vessel has just arrived from Jamaica, felt a violent bite in the lower part of the thigh, when he perceived a large centipede firmly adhering to his flesh. He called to some of the men, being too much shocked to touch the venomous reptile himself, who caused it to relinquish its hold, but not without some difficulty, as they wished to preserve it as a curiosity. The length of the creature was nearly ten inches. As the wound bled considerably, and the man felt in pain, he walked to the London Hospital, where the part was cut out to the extent of the circumference of a halfpenny, and half an inch in depth.

12 August 1841

EXTRAORDINARY CIRCUMSTANCE

There is a young woman of Abergavenny who, 16 years ago, unfortunately had a darning needle, and a piece of thread in it, thrust into her arm, and a few weeks since it came out at the ancle, the thread still in it; the needle was much smaller than when it went in, and considerably bent. During its passage from her arm to her ancle she never experienced any pain from it, but the leg is now very painful, being considerably inflamed. *(Preston Pilot)*

20 February 1843

STRANGE ACCIDENT

The wife of Mr. Strutt, the sexton of St. Peter's Parish, Colchester, had a narrow escape from death on Sunday week, by accidentally swallowing a wasp with some beer which she was drinking. The insect in passing down her throat stung it severely, without, however, leaving its sting in the wound; fortunately the wind-pipe escaped uninjured, or death must have ensued, but it renewed its attacks upon her stomach, occasioning great pain; medical aid was soon procured, and a powerful emetic, administered by Mr. Charles Murray, providentially effected speedy dislodgement of the wasp, though it was alive and vigorous when ejected from the stomach. *(Essex Standard)*

22 August 1846

SINGULAR ACCIDENT TO A SNIPE

A dead snipe was found lately in one of the Castle meads by Mr. W. C. Tisoe. It had evidently been starved to death with food in its beak. The upper part of its long beak was jammed

into a piece of hollow reed about an inch long, and in the lower part of the bill towards the point was enclosed a small beetle. The bird had no doubt been boring into the reed for the beetle, and the stump of a reed had broken, leaving a portion fitting so tightly round the upper part of the bill as not to be removed by any effort the bird could make. The bird has been stuffed by Mr. Knight with the beetle within, and the reed around its bill, as a curiosity. *(Hertford Mercury)*
29 March 1847

SINGULAR ACCIDENT FROM LIGHTNING

During the storm which passed over this town yesterday week a young woman named Stevens, living with Mr. Cater, butcher, in Magdelen-street, was struck by the electric fluid. She had retired to rest, and noticed nothing during the storm beyond being greatly heated; but upon rising on the following morning she discovered that the whole of her hair on the right side, and part on the back of her head had been burnt off by the lightning, the other portion being much singed. The left side was uninjured. It is regarded as a most singular circumstance that such an accident should have taken place without her having the slightest knowledge of it or feeling the least shock. The hair removed is about a foot long. *(Ipswich Express)*
26 May 1852

ACCIDENT TO PROFESSOR LIEBIG

The 'Augsburgh Gazette' has the following from Munich, dated the 10th:— "Professor Liebig was last night giving a lecture on chymistry at the palace, before Queen Maria, Queen Theresa, King Louis, the younger branches of the

7

Royal family, and some persons belonging to the Court, when a bottle of oxygen gas being improperly handed to him by his assistant, who took it for another bottle, an explosion took place, and the bottle flew into a thousand pieces. Fortunately, the explosion occurred in an inner room, the door of which was open; still some fragments of the glass passed through the door, and slightly wounded some members of the Royal party who were sitting in the front rank. Queen Theresa was cut in the cheek, and the blood flowed in abundance; Prince Luitpold was slightly wounded in the forehead, Countess Luxburg in the chin, and Countess Sandizell in the head. None of these wounds will be of any consequence. The professor was also slightly injured, having escaped with his life by a sort of miracle."

15 April 1853

DISTRESSING SCENE IN
ST. MARY'S CHURCH, LAMBETH

A very painful sensation was caused during the performance of divine service on Sunday forenoon last in the ancient church of St. Mary's, Lambeth. It appears that the Rev. W. D. James, the senior curate of the parish, was in the desk reading the morning service, when, on getting almost to the end of the Litany, a sudden scream was heard, and in an instant afterwards the rev. gentleman fell in his desk, apparently in a fit. The Rev. Mr. Easom, his brother curate, ran to his assistance, and succeeded in carrying the unfortunate gentleman into the vestry-room, where he was attended by Messrs. Sewell, Wagstaffe, and Collombell, surgeons, who were in the church at the time, and after some time he recovered sufficiently to be removed to his own residence. An apoplectic fit, it is presumed, was the cause of the rev. gentleman's attack. The remainder of the service was finished by the Rev. Mr. Sparkes, who alluded, in most feeling terms, to the melancholy scene the congregation had just witnessed.

25 January 1854

UNFORTUNATE AFFAIR

A sad mishap occurred a few days since at Portland, which occasioned no small degree of excitement from the peculiar circumstances attending it. A coastguardsman named Hansford had been frequently annoyed by a dog, the property of a farmer in the island, and he accordingly determined to shoot the offending quadruped. Armed with a loaded pistol, and attended by a companion, he sallied forth after dark to do the deed. On arriving at the spot of Snarleyow,* the coastguard, thinking he saw his game, fired off the pistol. Instead of hearing the yelp of the cur, however, he heard the groans of the companion beside him, for the ball had struck a wall opposite to them, and, rebounding, entered the neck of the unfortunate man, and passed down his side. Surgical aid was soon procured, but it was found that the bullet had made its way too near the region of the heart to allow of its being extracted. The poor fellow lies in a most precarious state. (*Wiltshire Mirror*)

31 August 1854

BALLOON ACCIDENT

An accident, the consequences of which are expected to be fatal, took place at Cannes on Sunday last. A M. Despleschin, of Nice, had announced his intention of making an ascent in a balloon, and two gentlemen, M. Hardy, of Cannes, and M. A. de Sorr, a literary man from Paris, had made arrangements to accompany him. These two gentlemen had taken their seats in the car, M. Despleschin not having yet entered it, when some person in the crowd, anxious to see the balloon start, cried out "Let go." The man who held the ropes, thinking that the order had come from the aeronaut, obeyed, and the balloon rose rapidly into the

---

* A reference to the popular adventure novel *Snarleyyow, or The Dog Fiend*, by Captain Marryat.

IT WAS ME WHO SHOUTED
'LET GO'. I CAN'T STAND
THOSE TWO!

M. DESPLESCHIN

clouds, and disappeared. M. Hardy and M. de Sorr are both entirely ignorant of the management of a balloon, and it is feared that they have been carried out to sea. Up to the 2d. no intelligence had been received of them.

9 May 1854

A STRANGE STORY

We learn from Captain Meyer, late of the schooner Falmouth, who arrived yesterday from San Quintin, in the schooner Frances Helen, the following account of a mutiny that occurred in the gulf of California at a recent date:—"The schooner Waterwitch, Captain Young, sailed from this port some time since, with an assorted cargo, for Colorado River, having on board the owners, Messrs Ames and Eliot. She proceeded up the gulf of California about 200 miles, where it seems there is a barren and uninhabited island. While off that place Captain Young remarked to the owners of the vessel that there existed a large marble quarry at that place, and proposed landing to examine it. Mr. Ames assented, and, together with the captain and the mate, accompanied by a large Newfoundland dog proceeded to the shore. The moment his companions left the boat Captain Young shoved off, leaving them, and returned to his vessel and put off to sea. Eliot, who was still on board, expostulated with the captain, when the latter drew his pistol and commanded silence; but, after some persuasion, Captain Young seemingly consented to return to the island and leave some provisions for those left behind. For this pretence he went ashore, taking Mr. Eliot along with him; but when the latter got on shore the captain shoved off the boat and left him, as he supposed, with the others. The former persons, however, on the departure of the vessel, had killed the dog, and, cutting his skin in strips, constructed a raft on which they embarked for the shore, some 15 miles distant, which they reached in safety. In the meantime, Captain Young had

11

shaped his course up the gulf, having for his crew one sailor and an Indian boy. The latter, overhearing the two former in conversation, learnt they intended to cut his throat, and throw him overboard, and proceed to Mulajoha Bay, where Captain Young intended to sell the vessel and cargo. After hearing this he quietly stripped off his clothes and dropped overboard and swam for the shore, about two miles distant, which he reached in safety. By this time Ames and his companions had reached Mulajoha Bay, when they gave notice to the officers of the place. Soon after the schooner hove in sight, and Captain Young landed, armed to the teeth, little dreaming that the news of his operations was in advance of him. As soon as he landed, he and his companion were arrested and put in prison. They are now on their way for this port on board the schooner Kate Hill, Captain Parker. As soon as they found Mr. Eliot was on the island, a boat was sent for him, and he was fortunately rescued from his perilous position. The Indian boy had also arrived at that place, having suffered considerably on his way."

9 January 1856

EXTRAORDINARY ACCIDENT

An extraordinary operation, necessitated by a singular accident, has just been performed in the Bristol Royal Infirmary. A young Irishman, named Patrick Haggarty, residing in New-street, St. Philip's, while romping with some of his countrywomen and neighbours, ran after a buxom girl, engaged in sempstress work, and gave her a hug in sport. It proved, however, anything but sport to him, for as he pressed the girl to his bosom, it turned out all but a fatal embrace, as a needle which was in the breast of her gown, literally entered the cavity of his chest, and broke off, leaving nearly three-quarters of an inch of steel in the muscles. Haggarty instantly felt sick and faint, and was taken to the infirmary, where it was determined to make an effort to ex-

tract the needle so as to prevent inflammation of the heart and death from ensuing. Dr. Green accordingly cut through the outer flesh, and laying bare the surface of the heart discovered a small portion of the needle fragment protruding, which he drew out with forceps. The delicate operation was most successful, and Haggarty, though not yet entirely out of danger, is progressing favourably.

3 June 1856

A TALE OF A TIGER

A few days ago (the narrative is in all the journals) a Bengal tiger, on its way from the docks, where it had been landed, to the premises of Mr. Jamrach, an importer of such luxuries, broke loose, and, after running crouchingly along the street, sprang upon a poor child, and mangled him cruelly. Mr.

Jamrach rushed to the rescue with a crowbar, and was dealing the savage animal a series of heavy blows, in order to deliver the boy, when the editor of a penny humanitarian paper came up, and begged Mr. Jamrach not to be hard on the poor beast, who knew no better than to mangle children, and had also a grievance in being restrained from his wild liberty. Mr. Jamrach rudely shoved the mediator out of the way, and, with a few more vigorous strokes discomfited the brute, and saved the child's life. The editor is virtuously indignant, and declares that Jamrach is no better than Havelock and Wilson.*

5 November 1857

Editors note: The Times has not always been noted for its accuracy. Other reports of this accident had appeared in The Times of the 27th and 30th October, describing the boy as the 'fearfully mangled little sufferer', and as lying 'in a very precarious condition'. This prompted the following letter from the surgeon treating him:

Sir, Owing to a paragraph which appeared in your impression of Tuesday, giving an exaggerated account of a singular accident which happened to a boy in Ratcliff-highway on Monday from the escape of a tiger from its cage, I have had inquiries respecting his condition.

I think it, therefore, only just to the public, through the medium of your columns, to state that the boy is not and never has been in danger from the injuries he then received.

He was brought here suffering from two small wounds in the arm, caused by the teeth, and a slight scratch on the scalp from one of the claws, of the tiger.

I am, Sir, your obedient servant,
Francis Owen, House Surgeon,
London Hospital.

---

* Gen. Henry Havelock and Sir Archdale Wilson, who distinguished themselves in the Indian Mutiny of 1857.

It is all the more surprising, then, to find the above account of the 5th November continuing to describe the boy as having been 'cruelly mangled'.

FIGHT BETWEEN A NEGRO AND A PANTHER

On Monday evening last an accident occurred in Edmonds' (Wombwell's) Menagerie, now exhibiting at Nottingham, which at one time wore a most serious aspect. "The Royal Lion Hunter", a native African, entered the performing panther's den. He then commenced to put one of these animals through a course of performance, which consisted mainly in making it leap from one platform to another, the two elevations being erected at either end of the den. The animal, instead of taking the proper course, leaped upon its keeper and tore his face, so that the blood ran copiously from the wound. The keeper, no ways daunted, notwithstanding a cry of terror from the spectators, persisted in making his refractory subject resume its position. For some time the beast continued obstinate, notwithstanding a terrible thrashing which it had received. The keeper then left the den, and, procuring a still heavier weapon, he returned and gave to the stubborn brute such a proof of his prowess as finally overawed it, and amid the applause of the spectators the performance went on, and was completed according to the programme before the keeper quitted the den, though all this time he himself was bleeding freely from the wound inflicted by the animal on his face. The self-possession of the keeper was highly extolled. The fight between the panther and his keeper lasted 20 minutes. The same evening a keeper went into the zebra's den, and while offering the male animal a biscuit it bit off his forefinger.

8 October 1862

EXTRAORDINARY ACCIDENT

On Friday afternoon, Mr. Samuel Angood, pawnbroker, of High-street, Lowestoft, was attending a sale at the Bell Hotel, Norwich, when a pistol belonging to him, being part of his stock of unredeemed pledges, was put up for sale, and while it was being held up for exhibition by a porter, named William Porrett, the man pulled the trigger, and the pistol went off. It appears that neither the porter nor Mr. Angood were aware of the pistol being loaded, and it must have been given into the custody of the pawnbroker when charged. The ball entered the left side of Mr. Angood's head, lodging at the top. Messrs. Frith and Drake, surgeons, were at once sent for, and they soon extracted the ball from the head of the sufferer. Mr. Angood is still at the Bell Hotel, and remains in a precarious condition.

14 August 1865

ENTANGLED IN A COW'S TAIL

A few days ago an inquest was held at Kelby on the body of Pearson Wakefield, aged 16 years. The deceased was in the employ of Mr. Everitt, of Kelby, and on the previous morning went as usual to a field about a quarter of a mile off to fetch up two cows to milk. He had been absent about 25 minutes, when one of the cows was seen running towards Mr. Everitt's farmyard, dragging deceased at her tail; and on being stopped the tail was cut, and deceased's leg, which had become entangled, was released. He was found to be insensible and severely bruised on the head and body, and died in half an hour afterwards. After hearing the evidence of the witnesses, the jury returned a verdict that deceased was accidentally killed. (*Armagh Guardian*)

8 November 1865

THE AGRICULTURAL-HALL

In the nightly programme of performances at Sanger's Circus, in the Agricultural-hall, is set down "The renowned Professor Palmer, as the Fly Man, performing marvellous feats of walking a glass ceiling." The professor has invariably walked the ceiling after fly-fashion successfully, but on Monday night he met with an accident which for the moment appalled the audience. The glass ceiling is composed of a piece of plate glass about 50ft. long by 20ft. wide, enclosed in a wooden framework. It is fixed at a distance of about 80ft. or 90ft. from the ground, and some 30ft. below it a net is spread to receive the professor in case of accident. On Monday evening the professor had taken his place on the ceiling, his feet being bound up in what appeared to be india-rubber, and commenced to walk, head downwards, on the glass, leaving on the latter as he lifted each foot a mark as if some glutinous substance had been applied to it. The utmost silence prevailed in the hall as he continued his perilous walk along the narrow glass, and all went well with him until within a couple of feet of the end of his journey, when by mistake he placed a portion of his foot upon the wooden frame instead of on the glass. His body immediately trembled violently, as if suction was the power which held him to the glass, and he struggled hard to keep up the weight of his body, which was now suspended from the glass by only one foot. His face, which up to this moment was very red, became pale, and in an instant the audience was shocked at seeing him fall head foremost towards the ground. The women turned their heads, and were afraid to look again at the spot, until a cheer reassured them. Palmer fell just on the border of the netting, which might well be of greater width. He came upon the back of his head, and having coiled his body into the shape of a ball, wriggled himself out of the net, and reached the ground by means of a rope ladder. Several gentlemen rushed from the front and second seats into the arena and shook hands with the professor, who then retired. He was called out again, and warmly applauded when he appeared in the circus, but he did not finish his performance. *31 January 1868*

EXTRAORDINARY ACCIDENT

On Saturday afternoon last a woman named Champion, the wife of a workman employed at the Cement Works, Borstal, was standing in her back kitchen, the door of which was open, when she suddenly found herself shot in the thigh, the rifle bullet striking the copper behind her. On finding herself wounded she at once went out of the house and informed Mr. Hopper and Mr. West, carpenters, who happened to be at work at some houses near, of what had occurred, adding, on their expressing doubt as to her statement, that she was quite sure she had been shot, as she felt the bullet pass through her thigh. As no person had been seen near with a gun, search was made in all directions to ascertain if any person had been using firearms, but to no purpose, as a careful examination of the adjacent fields failed to clear up the mystery. In the meantime Mrs. Champion became faint from loss of blood, and on Dr. Bell, surgeon, arriving, he ascertained that she had been shot through the thigh, as stated, the flattened bullet, which fortunately escaped the bone, being picked up close to the copper which it had struck. Not the slightest clue could be obtained as to the person who fired the gun, while, to render the matter still more inexplicable, no one in the neighbourhood could recollect having heard the report of firearms about at the time Mrs. Champion was wounded. On the following day, however, the mystery was cleared up, and the cause of the unfortunate occurrence ascertained. It would seem that Mr. Dalton, a member of the Volunteer Rifle Corps in this city, was on Saturday afternoon practising target firing at the range on Deloe Farm, Maidstone-road, and was in the act of doing something to his rifle, which was loaded, when, his fingers being smeared with oil, the hammer slipped from them, the rifle exploding in the air. It would now appear that it was this very bullet which occasioned the accident, the ball on leaving the rifle taking a curve over Cookham-hill, and falling at Borstal, a mile and a half distant, when it entered the open door, and struck Mrs. Champion under the circumstances related. Immediately on hearing of the accident on Sunday, Mr. Dalton felt that it was the stray ball from his rifle which had caused it, and stated what he knew of the circumstances. It is satisfactory to know that Mrs. Champion is progressing very satisfactorily.

19 October 1868

MELANCHOLY ACCIDENT

An extraordinary and melancholy accident happened last week at Retford, Notts to Mr. Henry Hutchinson, a veterinary surgeon, which unfortunately terminated in his death. The deceased gentleman was playing with two of his children, and having a dog's tooth in his hand he put it in his mouth. Suddenly, without thinking what he was about, he allowed the tooth to slip down his throat. At the time he thought very little of the occurrence, but finding that the tooth had not been altogether swallowed, and that it was beginning to pain him, he sought the advice of Mr. Marshall, who did all he could to reach it, but without success. Mr. Hutchinson was able to go about his professional duties until Thursday, when the tooth becoming more painful it was resolved to send for Mr. Barber, from Sheffield, to open the windpipe. Before this gentleman arrived, however, Mr. Hutchinson was dead. The affair has created quite a sensation in the neighbourhood. The deceased has left a wife and large family.

4 May 1869

FLY POISON

A singular fatality has occurred at Newmarket. A woman named Cooper, housekeeper to Mr. W. Boyce, was sitting near a table on which were some poisoned papers for the purpose of killing flies. A fly was seen to go to one of these papers and then to alight on the woman's nose, which was slightly scratched. The wound speedily became inflamed, in a short time her whole system became affected, and in about 24 hours the poor woman died.

3 September 1870

ACCIDENTS IN THEATRES

On Wednesday night during the performance of the pantomime of "Gulliver" at Sanger's Royal Amphitheatre (Astley's), an incident occurred which, but for the admonition which had been given to the densely crowded audience in the earlier part of the evening by Mr. George Sanger, might have led to some serious consequence, so great was the alarm it created. In the grand scene of the piece "the Palace of the Queen of Nations", where, in addition to the horses, there is a pageant including elephants, camels, dromedaries, and other Oriental animals, there seemed throughout an evident disposition, even on the part of the trained animals, to insubordination. The various cars drawn by the elephants, the camels, the giraffes, and the dromedaries came on in their turn, each led or mounted by a guide. One of the large dromedaries, the moment he came in sight of the stage with its gorgeous trappings on the one hand and the crowded house on the other, with the music of the band and the applause mingled, became restive, and a struggle ensued between the animal and its guide to get him into the place. The dromedary suddenly reared up, and, losing its balance, fell forward, rolled over towards the footlights, and for a moment it appeared inevitable that he would make his descent onto Mr. Sebold, the conductor, or some of his band, a general stampede of whom for a moment occurred. As may well be supposed, the excitement, especially among the female part of the audience in the pit stalls, into which the ordinary circus had been converted, was intense, and to add to it, almost at the same moment a shriek from the stage indicated that something had happened there also. This was simply that one of the female warriors borne aloft on shields in the pageant on the heads of negro slaves suddenly toppled over and came to grief. In the meantime the dromedary, who had been stopped from its descent into the orchestra by the brass rod which passes along the stage in front of the gas lights, had got its legs under it, and had managed to kick away the central limelight and all its apparatus, but it was forcibly dragged from its perilous position by the performers, under direction of Mr. George Sanger, and on resuming its proper place in the procession was received with a general burst of cheering. Its legs, however, must have had a very severe scorching. Mr. George Sanger, in pointing out to the audience the facilities for their exit in case of fire or any other calamity within the space of three minutes, also warned them not to be alarmed if they should at any time hear anything they might consider an undue noise behind the scenes, such as a few shrieks, as with an assemblage of 700 persons

22

engaged, the chief of whom were women and children, intermixed with the horses and other animals, such circumstance might occur without any danger, and from most frivolous circumstances. The performance subsequently proceeded to the end without the slightest further hitch . . .

29 December 1876

SINGULAR DEATH

The "Kölnische Volkszeitung" reports that at Rhode on Saturday evening, towards 7 o'clock, a priest was killed by a stroke of lightning in his confessional chair just as he was dismissing the last of the persons he had been confessing. This person was found insensible. The steeple of the church was also struck and burnt down. The church itself was uninjured.

4 July 1879

CAN'T UNDERSTAND IT. HIM AND THAT SNAKE WERE INSEPARABLE!

A FALL

Another edelweiss seeker has fallen a victim to his temerity. A young man from Lucerne, named Dabinded, was venturing too near the edge of a precipice on Mount Pilatus to gather one of the coveted flowers when he overbalanced himself and was dashed to pieces.

16 September 1879

A SHOWMAN KILLED BY A BOA-CONSTRICTOR

A lion-tamer, M. Karoly, who has recently been exhibiting before the public of Madrid his powers over the brute creation, had frequently performed with a boa-constrictor, the huge snake enveloping him in its folds, but never doing him any injury. On the last occasion he ever appeared the boa had, as usual, wound itself round the performer's body, when suddenly it tightened its folds. The spectators applauded, thinking it was some new trick, but Karoly simply uttered a groan, and in one or two seconds was a dead man.

6 October 1879

KILLED BY AN OSTRICH

Ostrich farming is not without its dangers as many a man has learned to his cost when sauntering among a flock of these birds without taking the necessary precautions against a sudden onslaught from a vicious member of the herd, but it is not often that we hear of a man being actually kicked to death by an ostrich. Such a fatality occurred recently in the district of Victoria, West Cape Colony. The bird had strayed on to

the public highway and disputed the progress of the unfortunate man to such purpose that he was kicked and trampled
to death. (*The Colonies and India*)

7 February 1882

FOX AND HOUNDS

A singular incident occurred in the last run of the Fitzwilliam
Hounds, which affords another illustration of the cunning of
the fox, and which placed the pack in considerable peril. The
"find" took place at Wadworth-wood, and the fox after heading for Rossington Station at a rattling pace, suddenly turned
in the direction of Loversall village, where he sought conceal-
ment in a bed of rushes near the Carrs. He was, however,
speedily compelled to quit his hiding place, and then made
again for the railway, where he deliberately lay down on the
permanent way and refused to budge. An express train was
rapidly approaching, and the pack, being in imminent
danger of getting upon the line and being cut to pieces, the
huntsman reluctantly and with considerable difficulty drew
off the hounds. The fox maintained his position until the
express got within a short distance and then quietly made off.

24 December 1884

ACCIDENT AT THE AMERICAN EXHIBITION

At the American Exhibition yesterday during the afternoon
performance of the "Wild West" show a serious accident
occurred to one of the principal characters – Buck Taylor,
"the King of the Cowboys". The fourth item of the programme consists of an attack by Indians on an emigrant
train, and the repulse of the attack by cowboys, the victory
being afterwards celebrated by a Virginian reel danced by

26

American girls and cowboys on horseback. It was in the course of the dance, apparently the gentlest and least hazardous of all the feats of Buffalo Bill's company from the Wild West, that the unfortunate *contretemps* occurred. When the reel was half finished Buck Taylor's sombrero suddenly fell off, and its owner was seen to sway to and fro on his horse for a few seconds and then to fall heavily to the ground, turning a complete back sommersault and afterwards lying still at full length. The spectators, not unnaturally, took this as a rehearsed effect until music and dancing stopped and Buffalo Bill and others dismounted and ran up to the injured man. A surgeon from St. George's Hospital happened to be among the spectators, and he at once rendered assistance, and under his direction Buck Taylor was borne from the arena in an improvised litter and at once conveyed to the St. George's Hospital. From the accounts of the other actors in the event, it seems that Taylor in reaching over for the hand of his partner during a sort of grandchain, lost for a moment the control of his horse, which swerved and brought him into collision with another rider, the projecting iron cantle of whose saddle struck Taylor's right thighbone just below the hip. The shock rendered Taylor insensible, his hands falling from the reins and his body swaying in a manner that at once attracted the attention of his comrades, although the public noticed nothing until he fell from his horse 30 or 40 paces from the point where the accident occurred. As soon as proper assistance had been rendered and the injured man had been removed from the arena the dance was continued and the programme brought to a satisfactory conclusion. The exact nature of the injury received could not be decided on the spot, though it was feared that a double fracture of the thighbone had been inflicted and that the consequences might be serious.

2 June 1887

ACCIDENT TO A LADY LION TAMER

There was an alarming occurrence in Mr. Dan Larry's Star Music-hall, Dublin, on Friday night. Mdlle. Senide, the lion-tamer, who for some weeks past has been exhibiting a troupe of wild animals, was taking her benefit. One of the feats she was in the habit of undertaking was placing her head within the mouth of one of her lions, and retaining it there for some time. When the entertainment was over, however, a photographer was in attendance to take views of her as she appeared in her performance. Two photographs of Mdlle. Senide with her lions were taken, and the third view was to consist of the lady in a cage with her head in the lion's mouth. It required a considerable time to arrange the preliminaries, and the lion, it appears, grew impatient under the delay. Meanwhile Mdlle. Senide was holding her head in the animal's mouth in the manner which she was in the habit of appearing before the audience, when the photographer turned on the magnesium light. The flash startled the animal, and he closed his mouth suddenly. Fortunately the lady was able to withdraw her head quickly, but her right cheek was caught by the teeth of the animal, and was torn completely open, the cut extending down to the chin. The animal also placed his paw upon her shoulder, and inflicted an ugly scratch along the upper part of the chest. The lion exhibited no anger, and after the occurrence crouched down in the corner of the cage. On Saturday morning Mdlle. Senide sent word by her manager that she would appear that night at the music-hall, but her doctors persuaded her not to do so. She is still thought to be in some danger.

6 February 1888

AN ACCIDENT TO A HINDOO
AND ITS CONSEQUENCES

The Indian papers report that some time since, in the neighbourhood of Fyzabad, a man of the Ahir or cowherd caste was carrying a young calf home on his shoulders, when by some accident it slipped down and broke its neck. The Brahmans declared him to be outcast and sentenced him to the severest form of Hindoo excommunication for six months. They further told him that he could not have committed a greater sin than causing the death of a cow, but, taking into consideration that he was an uneducated man, they had dealt very leniently with him. During the period of excommunication he was ordered to lead a life of mendicancy, and, with a rope round his neck and a portion of the calf's tail on his shoulders, he was to perform pilgrimages to different Hindoo shrines. The members of his family were forbidden to supply him with either shelter or food under a penalty of undergoing similar excommunication. The Ahir recently returned to his village, but until the purification ceremonies are over he must live in a temporary grass thatched house which has been erected for his residence. It remains for a man of one of the lowest and most degraded castes to purify him. A barber, after shaving the delinquent and paring the nails of his hands and toes, will make over the hair and nails to the low caste attendant, who will burn them and also set fire to the hut. After this the Ahir being covered with cow-dung, will take a plunge into the river Sarju and come out purified. But his troubles are even then by no means at an end. After he has feasted 50 Brahmans and 100 of his brethren he will be readmitted into caste-fellowship.

28 April 1892

The poignant . . .

A CRUEL CUT

Madame Bretot, a thriving blanchisseuse, of the Rue de Bièvre, had a fair daughter, who, like all her sex of the same age, which was tempting 18, was very fond of balls and other gaieties. The good mother was indulgent but prudent, and while she permitted her lively damsel to attend these scenes of amusement, always took care to accompany her. At a Sunday's dance, about a month ago, at the Quatre Saisons, Mademoiselle Eugénie met with a partner so genteel and gallant, that he won the hearts of both mother and daughter, and the favoured youth was received into their domestic circle as a suitor. The preliminaries were at length so far arranged for a marriage between the lovers that Madame Bretot drew 1,000 francs from the savings'-bank to purchase a suitable outfit for the young couple. Alas, for the uncertainty of human projects! Two evenings ago, when the expecting bride and her mother returned home, after a day spent on their knees, not at church, but in their wedding barge, near the Pont de l'Archevêché, they found that their dwelling had been broken open, their locks forced, and not only the 1,000 francs but every other article of value carried off. This was indeed a dire disaster, but the severest cut of all was a sheet of paper, conspicuously affixed to the chimney-glass, on which was written, in too legible characters, "I might have taken both your daughter and her dower, but I content myself with one, and leave you the other."
(*Galignani's Messenger*)

7 September 1841

30

SINGULAR FATALITY

A British soldier accidentally fell into the water at Quebec, Canada, a few days since, when a sentinel walking by attempted to get him out by reaching him the butt of his musket. The drowning man grasped the weapon, and in his struggles, it was discharged; the contents entered the head of the sentinel and killed him instantly. *(American paper)*

30 April 1845

TIGHT LACING

On Monday evening an inquest was held before Mr. Higgs, at the Coach and Horses, Avery-row, Bond-street, as to the death of Miss Elizabeth Allen, aged 22, a pupil of Madame Devey, of No. 75, Lower Grosvenor-street, the fashionable milliner. Mr. Robert Donett, of No. 6, Bruton-street, surgeon, stated that he was called in to see the deceased on Friday afternoon, about 5 o'clock, and found her quite dead on the bed, and very nearly cold. He was of opinion that she had died very slowly from the appearances about the mouth. He could discover no traces of poison about her or in the room. He understood that she had gone up to her room at 2 o'clock, after eating a very hearty dinner. She was of very full habit of body, had come up from the country, and was one of the finest young women he ever saw. She had been found by the side of her box, and he heard she was subject to fits. He had no doubt the stooping posture and tight-laced stays had brought on congestion of the vessels of the head, which, no doubt, was the cause of death. He had measured her corset, which was 1 foot 11 inches round, and on her body it would not meet in the smallest part by 2 inches. He was not aware if that was the usual way they were made, but if so, it was certainly too much contracted. The jury returned a verdict of "Died by the visitation of God."

14 August 1844

SINGULAR CASE OF DROWNING

A short time since Mr. Henry Ralph, yeoman, of Bagber, near Sturminster, Dorset, went to bathe in the river adjoining his farm. He was followed by his favourite dog, and as Mr. Ralph was swimming in the stream, the animal out of fondness for his master also took the water, and got on his master's back, which obliged him to turn himself over; and, when in this position, the dog again got on his bosom and neck, which caused his master to sink, to rise no more alive. A youth, a servant of the deceased, witnessed the sad catastrophe without being able to render any assistance. Mr. Ralph was a single man, and much respected by all who knew him. (*Bath paper*)

23 July 1847

SINGULAR OCCURRENCE

On Thursday morning one of those extraordinary beings who gain a precarious subsistence by penetrating into the sewers in search of coin or other valuables that may be washed into them from the drains was taken out of the main-sewer in Broad-street, Golden-square, in a very exhausted state, having been 36 hours and upwards endeavouring to find his way out, which, from having advanced further than was his custom to recover some silver that had been accidentally dropped down a grating near the Seven Dials, he was unable to accomplish. Fortunately, the poor fellow's cries were heard by Mr. Tickle, cheesemonger, at the corner of Berwick-street, Broad-street, opposite whose door there is a manhole, which he had contrived to ascend, and, assistance being procured, he was liberated. Some compassionate persons supplied him with soup, &c., which speedily restored him. *(Globe)*

1 April 1848

FATAL ACCIDENT FROM A PEA

A youth, the son of Mr. Richard Bolton, of Great Horton, Yorkshire, was playing a few days since with a juvenile companion, who was pretending to place a pea in his ear and to make it come out of his mouth. Bolton, believing the feat to have been really performed, was induced to make the attempt himself, and thrust the pea so far into his ear that it could not be got out. In a vain endeavour to extract it made by a medical man, it was sent further in, and the poor boy died four days afterwards from the effects.

27 November 1850

EXTRAORDINARY COINCIDENCE

A most extraordinary circumstance connected with the accidental death of a fisherman named Brat occurred at Plymouth on Friday. He was the master of a trawling sloop, and on the day in question was out in his vessel fishing, when he fell overboard and was drowned. About four hours afterwards his son, who was mate of another trawler, and who had not heard of the accident, was hauling up his trawl, which appeared unusually heavy. After some difficulty, however, the trawl was hove onto the vessel, and within it was discovered, to the consternation and dismay of all parties on board, the body of the mate's father.

6 August 1851

A ROBIN IN DIFFICULTIES

While Mr. Charles Newall, granite-hewer in Dalbeattie, was plying his vocation on Thursday last at Craignair Quarry, his attention was suddenly arrested by cries strongly indicative of distress proceeding from one or other of the feathered denizens of the wood. On throwing from him his tools and hurrying to the spot whence the sounds proceeded, he discovered a robin apparently in a state of the greatest agitation, whose movements immediately certified him of the true cause of the alarm. An adder 20 inches long, and one inch in circumference, had managed to drag itself up the face of the quarry, and was at that moment in the very act of protruding his ugly head over the edge of a nest built among the stumps of the cutdown brushwood, and containing poor mother robin's unfledged offspring – her maternal instinct prompting her to the only defence of which she was capable. She was engaged when Mr. Newall first got his eye upon her in alternately coming down the one moment upon the spoliator, darting her beak into his forehead, and anon rising on the other to the height of a yard or so above the scene of danger.

It was the act of a moment for Mr. Newall to dislodge the aggressor. But in doing so two of the little birds were thrown out of their nest, where, however, they were speedily and carefully replaced. While Mr. Newall was killing the adder, the joy of the parent bird was so excessive, that she actually perched on the left arm of her benefactor, and watched with an unmistakable and intense delight every blow inflicted by his right on her merciless and disappointed enemy; and when that enemy lay dead, she alighted upon and pecked the lifeless trunk with all her vigour, and, revenge thus taken, entered her nest, and having ascertained that all was safe, swiftly repaired to a neighbouring branch, and piped, as she best could, what was no doubt meant for a hymn of gratitude and a song of triumph. When at work since Mr. Newall has been evidently recognised by the tiny biped, and we do hope that nothing may occur to interrupt a friendship originating in circumstances so specially interesting. *(Dumfries Courier)*

4 June 1852

EXTRAORDINARY DEATH

On Thursday Mr. W. Carter, coroner for East Surrey, held an inquest, which lasted several hours, at Mr. R. Thomas's, the Holland Arms, Brixton-road, on the body of John Hanagan, a plasterer, aged 32. David Hanagan, the first witness called, deposed that he was a cousin of the deceased, who lived with his mother, at No. 36, Chapel-street, North Brixton. About five years ago the deceased was engaged in a fight at Woolwich, and received a severe blow on the throat, which rendered a surgical operation necessary. The operation was performed at Guy's Hospital, a silver tube being placed in his throat, through which he breathed, instead of through his mouth and nostrils; and when he wanted to speak he had to put his finger on the tube to prevent the air from escaping. He (deceased) had also a silver instrument, called a key, to keep the tube clean, but which he had lost about 12 months since. On Monday night last he (witness) had been drinking with the deceased at a beerhouse, when he appeared perfectly well. Witness, upon returning home, being rather intoxicated, fell asleep, but was shortly afterwards awakened by his aunt, who told him that the deceased was dying, and he immediately ran for a surgeon; but, on his return, he found he had expired. Mary Hanagan, the mother of the deceased, stated that on the night in question she told her son to go and "wash" (meaning to clean out the silver tube in his throat), for which purpose he retired into the back yard, but shortly afterwards came running in, saying, "Oh! mother, kiss me, for I am a dead man!" and immediately fell down and expired. By the Coroner:— He had been in the habit of cleaning the tube twice a day with the silver key, but since he had lost it had used a piece of stick instead. She was of opinion that while trying to clean out the tube the piece of wood had stuck in it. Mr. F. B. Gatty, surgeon, of 3, Elizabeth-place, Brixton-road, deposed that on Monday night last he was called upon to see the deceased, and, on his arrival, found him lying on the floor quite dead. Upon examination, he found he (deceased) had undergone an operation in the wind-pipe, and discovered in the opening a silver tube inserted, in which was a piece of willow wood, which he (witness) immediately extracted. Upon attempting to remove the silver tube he found that it had been broken in two. He was of opinion that death had been caused by some large artery being cut into, either by the piece of wood or by the broken portions of the tube. By the coroner:— The stick being in the tube would not of itself have caused immediate death. Sarah Hanagan, a sister of the deceased, aged 11 years, stated that she had often heard her brother remark that the pipe in his throat was nearly worn out, and that, if it once broke, he would be a dead man. The jury returned a verdict of "Accidental death."

1 January 1853

FATAL ACCIDENT TO A SLEEP WALKER

On Friday morning Mary Woods, aged 66, spinster, was
missed out of her bed, in the house which she occupied at
Liscard, on the Cheshire side of the Mersey. Some of the
villagers reported that at an early hour that morning they had
seen a figure dressed in white, and which they supposed to be
a ghost, walking in the direction of the ferry, and later in the
morning the body of the unfortunate lady was found floating
in the river, near the ferry, clothed only in her night-dress.
An inquest will be held on the body on Monday.

28 December 1857

LAMENTABLE AFFAIR

M. Emile de Vauxonne, Judge at the Court of Appeal, and President of the Council General and of the Municipal Commission of Lyons, went on the 25th to the shop of M. Gobert, gunsmith, to get a pair of pistols repaired. By an inexplicable chance it happened that the pistols were loaded, and on M. de Vauxonne touching the trigger of one of them to show M. Gobert what the pistol required, the pistol went off, and the charge struck the gunsmith obliquely in the breast. He at once fell on the ground, crying out, "I am a dead man!" M. de Vauxonne, horror-struck at what had occurred, seized on the other pistol and blew out his brains. When medical aid was brought to M. Gobert, it was discovered that the wound which he received is not likely to prove of any gravity. This fact renders the precipitancy of M. de Vauxonne the more to be lamented.

30 March 1853

MELANCHOLY ACCIDENT

Mr. Ouchterlony, of Goodaloor, not far from Madras, was walking with an attendant, his horsekeeper, with a rifle on his estates, on the 6th of December last, when the attendant went on in advance, thinking he saw a tiger. Mr. Ouchterlony took his rifle, and then crept till he got to some high grass, and through it to a favourable position in the grass, where he could watch any animals that might come into it. After a while a movement below attracted his attention. The grass moved, and there was a pause; a dark object was raised apparently towards the top of the grass, then it was depressed; and these movements, exactly resembling those of an animal in the grass, were repeated. At first it seemed to come towards him, and then to be turning away, when he

40

fired into the grass where it appeared to be. His horror may be conceived, when on making his way to the spot, he found that the shot had taken fatal effect on the unhappy horse-keeper. It had passed through the brain, and death had been instantaneous.

20 January 1860

A STRANGE STORY

A sad event, unfortunately not unique in the annals of science, has just occurred here. Some time ago a lady, of superior talent as governess in private families, had confided to her care a little Russian boy, born deaf and dumb. The child was of gentle temper and endearing manners, and the poor governess bent the whole of her intelligence to the possibility of instructing him to keep pace with her other pupils. Soon, at sight of his quick comprehension of the various methods she invented for his instruction, she began to grow more ambitious still, and to be devoured with the desire to endow him with the faculty which Nature herself had denied. For this purpose it appears that Mademoiselle Cleret spent whole nights in study, and lavished her slender means in experiments. At length the light broke in upon her. She remained perfectly convinced that in sulphuric ether must reside the talisman powerful enough to restore the deaf to a sense of hearing. She began by pouring into the ear a few drops only at a time, gradually increasing the quantity until it reached 10 drops. The cure was complete. The child heard and understood in a short time. The articulation was still imperfect for a little while longer, but that, it seems, has since yielded to surgical treatment. The fame of the cure spread far and near. The remedy was tried upon numberless individuals in all stages of deafness, and in every case succeeded. A commission was named to pronounce upon the discovery made by Mademoiselle Cleret. The decision was made wholly in its favour, the Montyon prize was awarded to the

41

fortunate lady, and various testimonials of favour were conveyed to her, both from public bodies and from private individuals. But the end of this sacrifice and devotion to the cause of humanity is sad to tell. Poor Mademoiselle Cleret, unable to resist the change from a position of dependence and privation to one of fame and comparative opulence, has sunk beneath the weight of the unexpected honours thus conferred upon her. Her mind, worn out with study and anxiety, worn out with labour and with watching, has given way, and she has just been conveyed a hopeless maniac to a maison de santé at Montmartre. *(Letter from Paris)*

1 May 1860

HANGED BY ACCIDENT

A very singular case of accidental hanging occurred in Cumberland this week, by which a boy named George Dodd, 14 years of age, lost his life. The deceased was employed in a coal pit near Brampton, Cumberland, and on Monday morning went towards the mine to his work in his customary good health. Shortly afterwards his father, missing him from his post, went into an adjoining stable to search for him. To his horror he found his son hanging by his neck suspended by a rope, quite dead. It appeared from the evidence taken at the inquest, which was held on Tuesday, before Mr. Carrick, the county coroner, that before commencing work on Monday, the deceased and some other lads had been amusing themselves with telling stories. Among others two were told of people being hanged by accident. One of these tales related to a lad who had tried to ascertain how long he could hang without a fatal result, and who had died before his comrades could rescue him. The other was of an acrobat, who had met with his death under similar circumstances. The deceased on hearing the stories, laughed at the idea of the boy not being able to release himself from the rope, and he no doubt then mentally resolved that he would try the experiment himself.

42

He did so, and was hanged. The jury took this view, and returned a verdict accordingly.

13 January 1864

EXTRAORDINARY RESCUE

On Tuesday last a gentleman named Woodward, a resident of Maldon, and who is blind, was bathing in the river Blackwater, the tide being at its highest, while at the same time a man named Perry, who was known to him, and a young man named Pearson, were bathing near. After they had been in the water a few minutes Mr. Woodward, knowing Perry was close by, called out to ask him where he was, but receiving no answer, and calling several times without success, he referred to his guide boy who was sitting on the bank, and, finding that Perry was not to be seen, immediately shouted for help. Pearson soon came up, when in answer to the excited inquiry of Mr. Woodward as to whether he could see Perry, he replied, "Yes, under the water, straight ahead of you." Mr. Woodward, guided by further directions, proceeded in search, and fortunately succeeded in reaching the poor fellow, and getting him safely to the shore. As it happened, it was providential that Perry was insensible, as had he had sufficient consciousness to have grappled with his preserver the result might have been fatal to both. It appeared that Perry, who can swim but little, got out of his depth, and, being crippled and weak from a late illness, was unable to help himself in the least, and doubtless was rapidly drowning. He has since been severely ill in consequence of the accident. It is an almost unparalleled case that a blind man should exhibit such presence of mind and tact as to be enabled by verbal directions only to find a drowning man, in so large an expanse of water especially, and unaided bring him to shore in safety. (*Essex Herald*)

31 August 1865

A LITTLE HERO

The 'Greenock advertiser' reports a remarkable instance of self-command and conscientiousness exhibited in the Glebe sugar-house on Thursday evening by a little boy of about 12 years of age, who fell into a syrup cistern, but managed to clamber out before those who heard his sharp shriek could get to his assistance. At the time he fell he was engaged in shifting the conductor from a full cistern to an empty one, and having lost his footing on the ladder was plunged headlong into the hot and nearly boiling liquid. On getting out he was covered all over with syrup, and was in an intense state of excitement and evidently severely burnt. A number of the men at once got hold of him for the purpose of affording him relief, but in an instant he slipped out of their hands, and, to their astonishment, replaced the ladder in its position, and refusing all help he insisted on completing his work, because he knew that if others unaccustomed to it attempted to change the conductor the liquor would be lost. He deliberately completed his task, and then put himself into the hands of his master and workmen, by whom his clothes were removed, and they then soothed him with oil. He seemed very much burnt. The conscientious attention to duty displayed by the little fellow while suffering excruciating pain excited the greatest surprise among the men who witnessed it, and his employers have presented him with a substantial mark of their admiration. His agility in escaping at once from the cistern prevented more serious injury, and by this time he is probably at work again.

10 October 1865

SHOCKING ACCIDENT

A sad accident happened on Wednesday at a place called Bissoe, a few miles from Truro, Cornwall. A boy named Simon Eslick, 9 years of age, was riding an old donkey, when the animal hearing the bray of its young offspring, which had strayed away, at once dashed off at full speed in search of the lost one. The poor lad was unseated, and his feet getting entangled, he was dragged after the donkey until both fell down a steep shaft of an abandoned mine and were killed.

6 July 1867

BURIED ALIVE

On Monday afternoon Mr. Browne, coroner, held an inquest at the Talbot Inn, Mansfield, on the body of an old man named James Thorpe, who was found buried in a rabbit-hole on Saturday last in Harlow-wood. The deceased, who was 67 years of age, was employed by Mr. Swift (wood steward to his Grace the Duke of Portland) to kill rabbits, and he left home early on Thursday morning for that purpose. Friday night coming, and the deceased not making his appearance, a search was made, and again renewed on Saturday, by deceased's son and three other men, when they discovered a man's legs protruding from a rabbit-hole in Harlow-wood, and on making an examination they found that a quantity of earth had fallen upon him. In about half an hour they succeeded in removing it and pulling the man out, when it proved to be Thorpe. He spoke once and then expired. The old man was in the habit of getting into the holes in search of rabbits. When taken out, a rabbit and a ferret were found grasped in his hand. The jury returned a verdict of "Accidentally killed".

15 January 1869

DEATH THROUGH FEAR

Yesterday morning Dr. Lankester presided over a jury at Middlesex Hospital for the purpose of investigating the circumstances connected with the death of Adela Weeks, aged 26, and her prematurely born female child, whose lives, as alleged, have been sacrificed through injuries received by a fall from a window at 71, Newman-street, Oxford-street, while endeavouring to escape from a deaf and dumb paramour who accompanied her home on the night of the 2d inst. The Rev. Mr. Smith, attached to the Association in Aid of the Deaf and Dumb, was present on behalf of the man implicated. Louisa Baker, servant to Mr. Bartlett of 71, Newman-street, said, when deceased and the deaf and dumb man came the latter made strange noises. This was about 20 minutes after they had been in the room. Deceased asked for a pencil and paper, so that they might communicate, as they could not understand each other. Witness sat at her window watching them, when the man appeared very violent, and made motions to deceased that he would cut her throat if she did not open the door. She then ran to the window, got on the sill, and asked witness to remove the plants. Witness removed two or three, when deceased stepped out of the room, having one foot on the window sill. She lost her footing on the sill as she was leaving, and fell. Witness had hold of her hand, but could not prevent her falling. Mr. Llewellyn afterwards broke open the door. After some further evidence a verdict of "Accidental death" was returned in both cases.

12 August 1869

DROWNED BY HIS DOG

Yesterday morning two young men named Bellis and Jones were rowing in a small boat in the Mersey, near Tranmere. Bellis had his dog with him. The boat capsized. Jones, who was a good swimmer, tried to save Bellis, but the dog mounting on Bellis' back bit Jones savagely every time he approached Bellis. The result was that the poor fellow was drowned.

8 December 1869

MR VALLANDIGHAM'S DEATH

The American papers received contain certain particulars of the death of Mr. Vallandigham. Mr. Vallandigham was engaged as counsel for the defence of a man named M'Gehan, who was charged with murder by shooting. The murdered man had been killed by a shot in the abdomen, and the defence set up a theory that the occurrence was accidental, and that the shot had been discharged from the man's own revolver as he was drawing it out of his pocket. Mr. Vallandigham's colleague in the defence expressed some doubt when they were alone as to the acceptance of this theory, whereupon the deceased said, "I'll show you in a minute." There were two pistols on the table, one of them unloaded. Mr. Vallandigham put one of these weapons into his pocket, and withdrew it hastily, with the muzzle turned towards his body. At that exact moment one of the chambers was discharged, the trigger having caught in Mr. Vallandigham's clothes, and he fell to the ground. The unfortunate advocate had demonstrated the reasonableness of his theory, but at the cost of his life; for the pistol which he had taken up was the loaded one, and the ball caused his death a few hours afterwards.

30 June 1871

A DANGEROUS CEREMONY

A correspondent of the "Nonconformist" writes:— "The Baptists in America frequently administer their dippings in what they call the 'apostolic mode', by making use of rivers for baptisteries. The dangers attending this system of baptism are sometimes very great, as is shown by the following newspaper paragraph:— Dr. A. P. Pownall, of Sand-hill, Kentucky, attempted last Sunday to unite with the Christian Church in that place by baptism. The clergyman, the Rev. J. B. Hough, led him out into the creek to a considerable dis-

47

tance in search of a spot of convenient depth, when suddenly both went down. They soon rose to the surface, and the minister regained the bank, but the doctor, being unable to swim, was swept by the current under a floodgate, only a short distance below. Every exertion was made to save him, but in vain. The body was soon after found and brought to shore, amid the most heart-rending screams from his young wife and friends. The doctor had been married but a few weeks to a Miss Mary J. Wilson, a greatly esteemed young lady of Sand-hill. When travelling in Sweden we heard of several persons who lost their lives in consequence of having been baptized in winter, the ice having had to be broken. In this case the fanatics who were guilty of the outrage were prosecuted and severely punished; and yet, when we returned to England, many Baptists of our acquaintance declined to believe in the truth of our statement of the facts, on the ground 'that no person could be injured by obeying the Lord's command'. We make a present of Dr. Pownall's case to such unbelievers, and sincerely hope that the days will soon come when such barbarities will cease in all parts of the world."

1 September 1871

SINGULAR FATALITY

On Saturday a singular case of accidental death was reported to Mr. John Humphreys, the coroner for Middlesex. Alfred Harris, aged 11, the son of a licensed victualler of Mortimer-road, Hackney, was in the habit of placing his head in a jack-towel hanging behind the door and swinging round and round until his head and face was enveloped as in a bandage. On Thursday last he again did it, but was seized with vertigo and hung senseless until he was suffocated. The poor boy was found dead hanging in the towel shortly afterwards.

19 April 1880

RUSSIA. ST. PETERSBURG: The following account of a sad accident, which is said to have occurred last Saturday, at Peterhoff, is circulating here, though I cannot vouch for its absolute truth:— The Emperor was out walking in the Park, and for some reason or other became interested in the operations of several workmen, or gardeners, who were at work at some distance off. His Majesty appears to have beckoned to one of the workmen to come up to him, intending to speak to the man, and perhaps, ask some questions. The workman noticed the sign, threw down his tools, and ran towards the Emperor. When only a step or two from his Majesty's person he fell dead at the Czar's feet, shot by a sentinel close at hand who had not seen the Emperor call the man and who had imperative orders to fire on any strangers approaching the Emperor. His Majesty, it is said, helped to lift up the body and showed the bitterest grief. The wife and family of the unfortunate man are to be thoroughly cared for.

17 July 1882

BAD LUCK, IGOR. HE WAS GOING TO BELT THE EMPEROR RIGHT ON THE HOOTER!

SWITZERLAND. GENEVA: On Saturday last a St. Gothard train was saved from what might have been a serious disaster by an act of rare courage and devotion on the part of a workman. As the noise of the train was heard in the distance, a large stone fell from the rocks above, at the outlet of the Polmengo Tunnel. A way guard who was on the spot, succeeded, by a great effort, in pushing the obstacle aside, but only by the sacrifice of his life, for at the same instant the train came up, and before he could get out of the way, he was caught by the locomotive and cut to pieces.

29 July 1882

THE UNITED STATES. PHILADELPHIA: On Thanksgiving night, Frank Frayne was playing in the Coliseum Theatre, Cincinnati, the Border drama, called 'Si Slocum', in which he shoots an apple from a girl's head. Owing to a fault in the spring catch of his rifle, Frayne missed the apple, and the ball entered the girl's head. She died 15 minutes afterwards. Her name was Annie von Behein, and she was engaged to be married to Frayne, who was almost crazed with grief. The play was at once stopped, and the audience, numbering about 2,300, were dismissed.

2 December 1882

FALL OF A CHERUB

An extraordinary and fatal accident happened this morning in the Roman Catholic parish church of Kildare. As the Very Rev. Dr. J. B. Kavanagh, P.P., was standing in front of the altar with his hand on the chalice to raise it at the close of 7 o'clock mass, and was about to descend the altar steps to recite the Rosary and Litany of the blessed Virgin, the marble figure of a cherub over the altar fell down and struck him with great force on the head. He fell back heavily, murmured the words "My God" twice, and then became insensible. A cry of horror and anguish was raised by the congregation who witnessed the accident. Some persons rushed forward to lift him up, while others ran for medical help. Drs. Watson, Dillon and Chaplin were soon in attendance, and Dr. Kavanagh having been raised from the floor was placed on a stretcher and carried into the adjoining convent, where, having never recovered consciousness, he died soon afterwards. The altar is a new marble one which was consecrated about a year ago with great solemnity by Archbishops Coke and Walsh. The tabernacle is surmounted by a spire-shaped canopy. The four pillars which support the canopy have corresponding short pillars above them, springing from each angle of the canopy, and on these are four cherubs. The one which fell weighed three stone. Great sympathy has been excited by the accident and the bells of the Protestant as well as the Catholic Church tolled mournfully during the day. Dr. Kavanagh officiated at the early mass this morning instead of his curate, because he intended to proceed to Dublin on business . . .

6 October 1886

The absurd . . .

ACCIDENT TO A PEER

At the coronation an accident happened to Sir Claudius S. Hunter. He made an effort to catch some of the coronation medals, which were cast about amongst the company. The other aldermen, however, were as anxious as he was to get hold of the coin, and in the experiment Sir Claudius, by some mischance, received a cut under the eye, and the blood streamed down. It happened, however, that Sir Astley Cooper was near the worthy baronet, and the blood was instantly stopped by Sir Astley without the use of lint or plaster. It was rather remarkable that some of the aldermen were fortunate enough to catch a medal.

10 September 1831

TRAPPED

A singular circumstance occurred at Brompton on Saturday, which, although it may appear rather ludicrous, was very near being attended with loss of human life. Apparatus has lately been constructed in Brompton church for the purpose of warming it with hot air; and as is customary, in order to guard against accident by fire, a wall was built around the furnace. The man employed in the structure, which is formed of bricks and Roman cement, continued steadily at his work by the light of a candle until it was complete, and it was not till he had inserted the last brick, and was as perfectly "built in" as ever an unhappy martyr in the days of persecution, that he discovered his error, and remembered that he was working within the circle instead of out. His first impulse was to pull out the last few bricks, and thus make himself a place of exit, but it was now too late, the cement had already hardened, and defied all his efforts to undo what he had already done. In this distressing dilemma he remained for a considerable time, calling in vain for help. His pitiable situation was at length discovered by one of the church-wardens and the sexton, who, after considerable difficulty, succeeded in extricating him from his imprisonment. The poor fellow's nerves were not a little shaken with the anxiety he had experienced during his incarceration.

17 January 1833

A SMART REMEDY

A few days since a boy belonging to the British school, Trowbridge, broke a blacklead or a slate pencil into his ear, and so far had it gone in, and still so short was the piece, that it bade defiance to the attempts of our eminent medical man to extract it, and a second would not make the attempt, but recommended the mother to take him to Bath, where he would at the hospital be sure to meet with proper attention, and be judiciously treated. Accordingly she was preparing the boy for a jaunt, and was performing due ablutions on his face, when the boy was not behaving quite so well as the mother thought he ought, she gave him a smart box with the palm of her hand on the ear (but not the ear which was affected), when, strange to say, out came the pencil! The cure was wrought as if by magic, the journey saved, and all by a good sound box on the ear. *(Bath Post)*

22 August 1839

GRAVESIDE CRASH

On Friday, as the clergyman was reading the burial service over the remains of the late Mr. E. Jenkins in Thorpe churchyard, the friends and family of the deceased standing round the grave, the sides of the pit suddenly gave way, and the whole of the party, together with the coffin, were thrown into the grave with a terrible crash. The circumstances of an event so appalling caused a deep shriek from the females present, but we are happy to say no person was seriously hurt. *(Lincoln Chronicle)*

23 September 1839

WAITED YEARS FOR THAT TO HAPPEN.
I CAN DIE HAPPY NOW!

55

PROVIDENTIAL FALL

The Rev. J. V. Stewart, vicar of Portsea, was a few days since exposed to the most appalling danger. He was standing on the vicarage lawn, near the open gateway, when an ox, in a state of furious excitement, rushed in, and made directly towards Mr. Stewart. The rev. gentleman, unprepared for such an attack, involuntarily raised his hand in his defence, the exertion of which, while standing on the wet grass, providentially occasioned him to fall down, and the infuriated beast went over him, without stopping to injure him. (*Wilts Independent*)

14 January 1840

ACCIDENT TO THE ARCHBISHOP OF YORK

On Monday last his Grace the Lord Archbishop of York left London for Sheffield, on his way to Ardsley, near Barnsley, to consecrate the new church recently erected there. On Tuesday the venerable prelate consecrated the church and churchyard, and afterwards held a confirmation at Ardsley, whence his Lordship proceeded, shortly after 2 o'clock, by railway, to the palace at Bishopsthorpe, accompanied by the Rev. W. H. Dixon, one of his Grace's chaplains. Before dinner the Archbishop took a walk into the fields in the vicinity of the palace, accompanied by Mr. Dixon, and as they were crossing an ancient drain, arm in arm, the united weight of the two gentlemen caused the arch of the drain to give way, and they were both instantly plunged into the filthy water and mud beneath, almost up to their chests. Fortunately, Mr. Egerton Harcourt, one of his Grace's sons, who was walking at a short distance in the rear of the two rev. personages, witnessed the occurrence and immediately hastened to their assistance. Owing to the perpendicular construction of the drain their release was a matter of some difficulty; but we are happy to say that it was effected without any other

57

injury, either to the venerable prelate or to his chaplain, than what may arise from their sudden and involuntary immersion. After undergoing the requisite lustration and changing his apparel, his Grace partook of dinner as usual, and was, we understand, not a little jocose upon the consternation which their sudden intrusion into the domains of the frogs and tadpoles, must have occasioned to the reptiles in the vicinity of the accident. His Grace consecrated the new church at Clifford on the following day (Wednesday); and we are glad to be able to say that at that time his Grace had not experienced any unpleasant consequences from the accident. (*Leeds Intelligencer*)

14 June 1842

"GOING BACKWARDS"

It is the proud office of the Duke of Argyll to bear the crown of England before the Sovereign on state occasions. However, it is not etiquette for the subject to turn his back upon his Monarch; though history shows us that this has been done too. However, in the prorogation of Parliament, the Duke of Argyll, carrying the crown and going backwards, slipped down two stairs, fell, and down, with a crash, fell the crown of England. Several of the diamonds were knocked out of the crown, and dukes and marquisses were picking them up like so many Sinbads. The Duke of Wellington, we learn, immediately became the historian of the fall of the crown, and in his own short-sword way narrated the mishap to the peeresses. Fair cheeks became pale, and many and eloquent were the "dear me's!" However, when the Queen quitted the throne, "the housekeeper appeared in front of it, thus taking charge of the position." We know not wherefore; for who in the House of Lords would have pocketed the Crown jewels? However, even among peers, housekeepers we suppose ought to be cautious. At length all the jewels were found, and the crown sent to be repaired, no doubt to the loss of Mr Swift, of the Tower, who shows it; for sure we are that

58

in its battered state people would have given an extra 3d. to see it: there is something so attractive in the misfortunes of the great. However, our chief business is not with the accident, but to suggest that every means be taken to prevent a recurrence of the calamity. It is plain that the education of the Duke of Argyll has been sadly neglected. Peers and others destined to play parts in a Court, ought from their earliest infancy be taught to walk backwards; to ride backwards; if possible – and it is possible we know – to think backwards. We have wet-nurses and dry-nurses; we ought to have nurses for the backward step. A proneness in a noble child to walk forward like a mere human animal should be repressed with the same anxiety that we now watch a tendency to bandiness. In fact, better be bandy than forward. To be an extraordinary backward child ought to make the best praise of a courtier in short clothes. And these lessons in backwardness we would have so given that they might visibly associate with them the person of the Monarch. Thus we would have the royal portrait in every nursery, that the children might play at ball and battledore and shuttlecock, always backing from the regal countenance. Or, as the good Mussulman always says his prayers with his face to the east, the backward pupil might be taught the various situations of the various palaces, and always reverently face the one whereat the Royal standard should be flying. We are very earnest in this matter. For is it not a sad thing that an elderly gentleman should be called upon to walk in a way that, when God made man, it was never intended that man should walk! Hence this fall of man, or fall of duke! There are, we know, hasty thinkers, superstitious quidnuncs, likely to predict some evil, to see a bad omen in this accident to the English diadem. Crowns have, we know, been shivered by going backwards, but that – despite the mishap to the Duke of Argyll – that can never happen to the crown on Queen Victoria. Nevertheless, we hope, for the sake of all parties, that those who shall henceforth convey the crown, will be allowed to go forwards. Then, certain we are, the crown will lose no one of its jewels. The olden bigotry may love the back step; but the spirit of our day cries – "Forwards!" (*Punch*)

21 August 1845

LOT No. 2. A VERY NICE LITTLE ALCOVE CONTAINING TWO GENTLEMEN

A CRASH

On Friday, as Mr. John Fullalove, auctioneer, was selling on behalf of the Salford corporation the building materials of a tenement at the corner of Norton-street, Greengate, which is to come down, for the purpose of improving the radius of the corner, having finished the sale of the ground floor, the auctioneer and his customers ascended to the first floor, and on his "knocking-down" the floor to some ill-starred purchaser, down it went in obedience to the hammer, carrying with it to the floor below upwards of 30 persons. Great was the confusion; some who were standing near the windows sprang out; two gentlemen who were standing in a small recess of the wall found themselves suddenly isolated, left standing alone on a small fragment of the floor; another hung for a short time, suspended by his hands from a sort of window called a Yorkshire light; but, with these exceptions, all the assemblage, including the auctioneer, had a taste of the 'facilis descendus'.* Mr. Fullalove had his clothes torn and one knee cut; Mr. Nelson, a builder, received some injury by a beam falling on his thigh, but, after having had medical assistance, he returned to the premises, and some others received bruises and slight wounds, but, fortunately, no one sustained any serious injury. *(Manchester Guardian)*

29 June 1847

AN ABSURD FEAT

The weekly return of the Registrar-General for the week ending April 8, reports the following decease:— In St. George's Hospital, a coal-porter, aged 24, died from haemorrhage from the internal carotid artery, consequent on a burn of his mouth and throat, caused by a red-hot poker forced into the mouth by falling while carrying the poker between his teeth as a feat. Three days elapsed between the receipt of the injury and the death. *(Globe)*

20 April 1848

* A reference to Book VI of Virgil's *Aeneid* ('Facilis descensus Averno' – 'Easy is the way down to the Underworld').

61

A DANGEROUS MISTAKE

On Monday last a collier, working in the Pentrefelen pit, near Llangafelach, nearly met his death under the following singular circumstances. He had brought with him a supply of food for his meals – among other things a pot of good strong tea – that famous plant "which cheers but not inebriates." In a similar pot he had with him a more dangerous companion, a pound and a half of powder – not the tea called gunpowder – but good rock powder, used for blasting purposes. At the usual hour for the meal the canny man took up the pot and set it on the fire. It was the pot of powder, not tea. The result may easily be imagined – an explosion, which burnt the man and a boy, and five who were at the time in a shed near the works with him. Fortunately the injuries received by the sufferers, though severe, are not such as to endanger their lives – a circumstance which they owe, in great part, to the shed being open, and the roof, we believe, partly uncovered. (*Welchman*)

30 October 1848

SINGULAR OCCURRENCE

On Tuesday week, as the coal train on the Swannington line was proceeding to Leicester, and when near Glenfield, the engine-driver suddenly perceived a fine bullock appear on the line, and turn to meet the train, head to head with the engine. The animal ran directly up to its fiery antagonist, and by the contact was killed on the spot. There was no time to stop the train before the infuriated beast came up. It was afterwards discovered that the animal belonged to Mr. Hassell, of Glenfield, and made its way on to the line from the field adjoining. (*Leicester Journal*)

10 August 1849

STRANGE ACCIDENT

A deplorable accident took place on the 13th at Oran on the exercise ground of the garrison. Some of the soldiers having seen a snake in the grass pursued it, and the reptile, in order to escape, crept into a cannon which had been left there since the last time the artillery were firing at a mark. The men, not supposing that it was loaded, determined to smoke the snake out of its hiding place. One of them accordingly thrust some lighted material in at the end, whilst another put down a lighted stick into the touch-hole. The piece at once went off, killing one man and wounding three others more or less severely. These latter were taken to the hospital, where hopes were entertained of saving their lives.

28 September 1850

AERIAL MISADVENTURES

On Saturday, at the moment of the Prince President's arrival, M. Toutain ascended in his balloon from the Hippodrome, from the car of which was suspended a large eagle, with extended wings made of wicker work, and which, when at a certain height, he was to have lowered down to a certain distance, when it would have the appearance of a live bird floating in the air. Unfortunately, the aeronaut was not provided with a pulley, so as to allow it to descend gradually, and he was therefore obliged to let the cord run through his hands. The friction was so violent that the skin was completely burnt off his hands, which are in such a state that it will be a long time before they are healed. On the same day M. Buislay, while performing his gymnastic exercises, in walking up an inclined plane on a ball, fell from a height of only about six feet, and fractured his shinbone so severely that it is thought he will never be able to resume his gymnastic performances.

21 October 1852

ACCIDENT TO SIR ROBERT PEEL

We regret to learn that the absence of Sir Robert Peel from the House of Commons on Monday night arose from the right hon. baronet's being confined to his residence by the effects of an accident which might have been far more serious than it has turned out. We hear that while dressing in the morning, he incautiously rested his foot on a china basin, and by the weight of his person the bottom broke, and severely lacerated his foot. Sir Benjamin Brodie was instantly sent for, and was as promptly in attendance on the right hon. baronet. Although the blood was profuse from the wounds inflicted, we are happy to hear that Sir Benjamin Brodie, after a minute examination of the injured parts, pronounced that no danger was to be apprehended, as not any important vessel had sustained injury. The casualty will necessarily confine the right hon. baronet some days to the house.

15 July 1846

FATAL RESULT OF MORMON FANATICISM

During several successive days a number of men have been engaged in searching the Trent between Nottingham and Beeston for the purpose of finding the body of a young man named William Barnes, recently a resident in the last named place. Barnes having latterly distinguished himself as a zealous partisan among the Mormonites, who unhappily are becoming rather numerous in and around the county of Nottingham, had been elevated to the rank of a priest or prophet. In this capacity he was about to receive a couple of converts into the bosom of "the church" on Wednesday night, at 10 o'clock. The "priest", the candidates, and a number of "brethren" approached the left bank of the Trent at the time named, the spot selected being in a place known as the Rye-fields, near Beeston. The converts, both young women, hesitated about going into the water, being fearful of danger, but Barnes bravely led the way, assuring them that no harm could befall the faithful. He had scarcely uttered some expression to this effect, and was stepping into the stream, which was unusually high and the current very strong, when in a moment he was carried off his legs and sank directly. One of the "brethren" with him, who could swim well, plunged after the unfortunate man, but was unable to reach him, and his body has never been seen since. The enthusiasm of these wretched fanatics is astonishing. They are constantly engaged in making proselytes, and many families have already been induced by their agency to leave this neighbourhood for the Mormon settlement in California.

3 February 1852

SINGULAR OCCURRENCE

On Sunday morning last a most singular accident happened at Monk Bretton Church. It appears that on the Rev. A. Lambert taking his place at the communion table, for the purpose of administering the sacrament, and on the wife of Mr. Thomas Wandsworth, who was the first communicant, kneeling down, the floor beneath her gave way, and the lady suddenly disappeared. The consternation, as may be imagined, was very great. Assistance, however, was instantly rendered, by putting a ladder down the hole, and happily the lady was found at the depth of eight feet uninjured, which was most providential, as the floor consisted of large stone flags, which fell to the bottom of the place. The accident was occasioned by dry rot having taken place in the timber that supported the raised floor, there not having been any ventilation provided beneath it.

24 February 1853

FATAL FALL FROM A CLIFF

On Thursday afternoon a large party of friends, who had been enjoying themselves at a picnic in the picturesque neighbourhood of Boscastle, Devonshire,* were about to return home, when the hat of Mr. Dennis, a solicitor, who was assisting two ladies to the carriage, was blown off, and, in running hastily to recover it, the unfortunate gentleman fell over the cliffs, and was instantly dashed to pieces. The deceased gentleman was much respected.

1 September 1853

* Actually Cornwall.

POISON SWALLOWED AT AN AUCTION

A few days ago, at a sale of the calico-printing materials of Mrs. Hulme, of Spring-vale, near Stockport, while some liquor called "dung-substitute" was under the auctioneer's hammer, a man said, "Let's have a look at that stuff!" and a small cup, in which about half-a-pint had been handed round as a specimen, was given to him. To the surprise of the company assembled he drank a small quantity, and then began to spit some of it out, saying it was "awful bad stuff," but, as it then appeared to have had no effect upon him, and as no one probably thought he had taken enough to harm him, he was only laughed at, and the sale went on. "Dung-substitute", however, is a mixture of deadly poisons, containing arsenic, white lead, and other deleterious articles (now used by calico-printers in place of cowdung), and in the course of the evening the man, who was a broker from Ratcliffe-bridge, was seized with dreadful pains, and died nine hours after taking the stuff in great agony. Medical aid was obtained for him, but without avail.   *28 March 1855*

A REGULAR FIX

During a thunderstorm in the town of Berne, says the 'Albany Knickerbocker', the electric fluid struck an apple tree, against which a young man named Lawrence was leaning. It split the tree from top to bottom, making a gap sufficiently large to let Mr. Lawrence slip in about a foot, immediately after which it sprung to, and held him tight as if he had been in a steel-trap. Before he could be extricated a resort to axes and crowbars became necessary. This is probably one of the tightest places that Mr. Lawrence ever got into.

18 September 1856

SINGULAR CASE OF POISONING

An inquest was held on Saturday evening at the residence of Mr. Thompson, a retired tradesman living in Rhodes-street, Halifax, on the body of Mr. James Thompson, aged 30, son of Mr. Thompson, who had died in consequence of taking a large dose of ammonia. The deceased had been in a low desponding state for two years previous to his death, and he had refused to take any medicine save what was given him by Dr. Garlick, the medical attendant of the family. About three weeks since some ammonia was purchased by Mrs. Thompson, who intended mixing it with water and then bathing her temples with it. The deceased got hold of the bottle, and, expressing a belief that that was just the medicine that would cure him, he was about to drink off a wine-glass full of the poison, when the servant came into the room and took it from him. The ammonia had since then been locked up in the cellar, but on Saturday morning the servant inadvertently left the key in the cellar door, and the deceased seeing it, and knowing the drug to be kept in the cellar, procured the bottle, from which he drank a large draught. He expired in a quarter of an hour afterwards. The jury returned a verdict to the effect that the deceased had drunk the poison under a singular belief that it would do him good.

21 April 1857

ICE-BOUND

On the evening of the 24th ult. the attention of some persons was attracted to an object in a pond in a brickyard near Barnsley. On proceeding to examine it they found a man up to the neck in water, with a collar of ice round his neck, which kept him fixed as in a vice. He was taken out quite insensible, and prompt efforts were made to restore him, but four hours elapsed before he recovered. He turned out to be a blacksmith from Silkstone, and he had fallen into the pond while returning home in a state of intoxication.

2 March 1858

A MAN CARRIED AWAY BY A KITE

A young man named Power, residing at Castlecomer, went a few evenings ago to fly what he termed a Spanish kite, of very large dimensions. Having adjusted the cord and tail, it rapidly ascended with a brisk breeze until it had taken the full length of the cord, which became entangled round Power's hand. The wind increasing, he was drawn a distance of nearly half a mile in the greatest agony, the cord cutting into the bone. The Rev. Mr. Penrose, the protestant curate of the parish, seeing the man running and shouting, at one time raised off the ground for a distance of some perches,* and again running along at full speed, perceived that he was dragged by the kite, and followed him as fast as he could; but

* A "perch" is equal to 5½ yards.

being unable to come up with him, he shouted at the top of his voice to "Let go; there was a man killed in a thunderstorm by the lightning of a kite." When Power heard these words, he shouted with redoubled vigour, but could not extricate himself until, after the distance mentioned, he was stopped by a high stone wall, the top of which, being coped, cut the cord and set at liberty the kite and the owner, who was almost lifeless with fatigue and fright. (*Kilkenny Journal*)

28 October 1858

MELANCHOLY DEATH

Intelligence has just been received in Newcastle-on-Tyne of the death in South Africa of Mr. John Burgess, a young gentleman who was born and resided for some time in that town. It appears that Mr. Burgess, who has been living for several years at the Cape of Good Hope, left Hopetown,

Orange River, in May, 1860, on an expedition to the Zambesi, where he expected to meet with Dr. Livingstone. He was accompanied by several Europeans and a number of natives. The party had three waggons, each of which contained a large quantity of gunpowder. All appears to have gone on well until the 22d of August, when the travellers neared a small river, known as the Sebluanie, in the neighbourhood of Moselekatse's country, where the waggons were drawn up side by side for mutual protection. Mr. Burgess, who had been hunting elephants all day, came in tired, and, contrary to his usual custom, retired to one of the waggons to smoke and rest, leaving the other Europeans sitting round the fire. Scarcely two minutes after leaving them a terrific explosion took place in the waggon in which Mr. Burgess was, which killed instantly that unfortunate gentleman and two of the natives, and more or less injured the rest of the party; seven horses were killed, and of the waggons only one front axle remained. Mr. Burgess was only 25 years of age; he had been eight years in the colony, and was greatly esteemed by all who knew him.

25 March 1861

SINGULAR ACCIDENT

An unfortunate accident has just occurred in the studio of M. Dubray, statuary, at Passy. That artist, to whom are due the well-known statues of General Abbatucci at Ajaccio, Jeanne Hachette at Beauvais, and the Empress Josephine at Martinique, which last work was seen in the exhibition of 1857, has just terminated, after a year's labour, the model of an equestrian figure of Napoleon I, destined for the city of Rouen. The committee charged to report on the work had willingly accepted the statue, being satisfied that a sculptor had never been more successful, and the casting of the work in bronze was decided to take place immediately. The Prefect of the Seine-Inférieure, attracted by the report of the com-

PERHAPS IT WAS FOR THE BEST. I DON'T THINK YOU QUITE CAPTURED THE SHAPE OF HIS NOSE..
NAPOLEON 1
ON HIS HORSE
M. DUBRAY

mittee, called on the artist to see the work, and the statue was being turned on its axis to exhibit it from different points of view, when the bar of iron by which the whole mass was supported suddenly broke in two, and the work was precipitated to the ground, rider and horse being reduced to a thousand pieces. It is impossible to depict the consternation of all present, but after the first emotion was passed M. Dubray announced that he should commence that very day on the work of preparing a new model.

14 May 1864

FATAL OCCURRENCE

On the evening of Tuesday, the 6th inst., Mr. Jameson, spirit-dealer, was sitting in the house of Mr. Parker, spirit-dealer, Waterloo-street, Kilmarnock, discussing a "friendly glass" with Andrew Isset, collier, and Mr. M'Millan, spirit-merchant, Glasgow. The conversation had turned on natural history, and while discussing the peculiarity of only the lower jaw in man being used in eating Mr. Jameson made a bet that he would put his thumb in Isset's mouth, and by holding his lower jaw prevent Isset from biting the thumb. It is alleged that at first Isset declined, but on being again asked he acceded to Jameson's request. Isset tried to bite the thumb once, twice, but did not succeed. On the third attempt Isset made a snatch at Jameson's thumb before he could get a firm hold of his jaw, and bit the thumb at the first joint. Next day the same party met again in Parker's, and after taking some liquor they hired a machine to convey Isset home. On Thursday morning Jameson's hand swelled to some extent, and Dr. Aiken was called in, who examined the hand. No decrease in the swelling taking place, Dr. Aiken called in Dr. Paxton to assist him, when the symptoms began to assume a serious aspect. The disease had spread up the arm, and it was cut in several places to try and confine the mortification, for such it appeared to be, to that part of his

body. On Thursday the doctors gave their opinion that Mr.
Jameson could not be expected to live long. This information
was conveyed to Mr. Gross, fiscal, and that gentleman, in
presence of Sheriff-Substitute Norrie, Captain Galt, Mr.
Fulton, Sheriff-Clerk Depute, and Drs. Aiken and Paxton,
took the dying declaration of the unfortunate man. On
Friday he gradually sank, and at 10 o'clock he expired.
The matter is being thoroughly investigated by the Crown
authorities.

21 December 1864

SINGULAR ACCIDENT

On the last day of the season of the B.V.H.,* Press, the
huntsman, took up the fox, which was apparently dead,

* The Belvoir Hunt.

76

when the "varmint" made a grip at his leg and caught him in the upper part of the thigh. Some hounds rushed up at the time and tore the fox away, buckskin and all. Luckily the seizure of the fox had compelled it in part to open its mouth, or some part of the huntsman's leg would in all probability have accompanied the piece of his breeches. Still he was wounded, but is now doing well.

10 May 1865

AN ADDER

On Saturday three men, named W. Perfitt, J. Lane, and J. Andrews, who had been bitten by an adder, were admitted under the care of Mr. Treeves, house surgeon at St. Thomas's Hospital. On the previous night, while at the Cooper's Arms, Portland-street, Walworth, Perfitt drew from his pocket what they supposed to be a snake, which they had picked up on Hayes-common, where they had been on an excursion, and suddenly found himself bitten in the left thumb. Perfitt threw the reptile on the table, and both his companions, in endeavouring to capture it, were both similarly bitten. It got on the floor, and a dog, in attempting to seize it, was bitten in the breast, and immediately commenced howling and swelling to such an extraordinary size that it was thought necessary to destroy it. The light then broke in upon them that they had been bitten by an adder, and they were conveyed to the hospital, where Perfitt and Lane still remain seriously ill. Andrews has nearly recovered.

31 August 1865

ABORIGINAL SPORTS

At an exhibition of native Australian sports by the aboriginal cricketers, at Bootle, near Liverpool, on Saturday, a

NATIVE AUSTRALIAN SPORTS

2. THROWING THE KANGAROO

boomerang, thrown by Mullagh, was carried by the wind among the audience. It struck a gentleman on the head, the brim of the hat saving the face from severe laceration. As it was, the boomerang cut through the hat and inflicted a severe wound across the brow. Surgical aid was at once procured, and the gentleman was able to return home.

14 September 1868

GUN ACCIDENT

A singular gun accident occurred at Pain's-hill house, near Cobham, the residence of Mr. Leith. The farm bailiff, Mr. Heal, laid a loaded gun on top of a corn bin in the stable, and to his great surprise he heard it some time afterwards go off. The gun was fired by a fowl which got upon the trigger, and the contents entered the face of a man named Collis, who happened to be in the stable at the time, inflicting very severe injury. The sufferer was attended by Dr. Webb, who was obliged to remove one of the eyes of the injured man.

25 August 1876

A MAD BULL

On Wednesday afternoon an extraordinary occurrence, unfortunately attended with fatal results in the case of one person, happened in Salford. A bull was being driven from the Cattle-market along the Crescent by a man named Leech, a butcher at Heywood, and another man named Job Ellison, residing in Rochdale-street, Heywood. When passing Peel-park the animal became frightened and ran at an omnibus, and subsequently at a lorry, which it attempted to upset. It next charged a handcart which was standing near the pavement and tossed it in the air. The bull then lay down in the roadway, and Leech was standing near it when it suddenly rose to its feet and knocked him down, inflicting slight injuries, which were dressed at the Salford Hospital. The animal turned into Adelphi-street, pursued by two police officers named Lane and Minogue, the first-named being armed with a revolver. Coming up with the bull, Lane fired one barrel at it, the bullet striking it upon the horns. The effect of the shot was to further increase the fright of the animal, which ran along Silk-street and Arlington-street, knocking down a man named James Roberts, a wood-turner, living in Back Silk-street, and a boy named Ralph Thomas-Yates, aged six years, the son of a joiner residing in Arlington-street. A man named Bradshaw was also knocked down, and somewhat severely injured. Roberts, who is a married man, was badly wounded and bruised, and sustained a cut on the right eye and internal injuries. He was conveyed to the Salford Hospital, where he received medical assistance, and was afterwards removed to his own home. The boy Yates was driven by the bull against a wall and wounded by the animal's horns in several parts of his body. He was removed to the Salford Hospital, where his wounds were dressed, and then to his father's house, where he died at noon yesterday. In the meantime the officer Lane had handed the revolver to a man named Fay, living in Ann-street, Adelphi. Fay aimed at the bull and fired; but the shot, unfortunately, missed, and passed through the shop window of 64, Silk-street, occupied by a provision dealer named Buckley, and struck Mrs. Buckley, who was standing behind the counter, in the right shoulder, lodging in the bone. Ultimately Police-constable Ormsby procured a rifle, and succeeded in killing the bull . . . (*Manchester Guardian*)

29 December 1876

A MADMAN'S FREAK

Last evening, between 7 and 8 o'clock, a man, evidently insane, climbed the railings and mounted the dilapidated statue of Queen Anne in front of St. Paul's Cathedral, and with a hatchet dealt several violent blows upon the face of the effigy, occasioning much damage. A crowd assembled, and it was not without difficulty that he was got down and taken to the police-station. He will be brought up at the Mansion-house Justice-room to-day.

7 February 1882

CHARGE OF MANSLAUGHTER

On Sunday night, at Farnworth, near Bolton, an elderly man named Walker was paying his addresses to a woman named Stafford, when her father, over 70 years of age, who was opposed to the intimacy, finding them talking together made some offensive remarks. They fought but were separated.

Stafford was carried into his house insensible, and died almost immediately. Walker was arrested, and on being charged he admitted having kicked the deceased once.

8 July 1884

ACCIDENTALLY SHOT DEAD

Samuel Halliday Smith, aged 15, a son of the Mayor of Bradford, was yesterday afternoon shot dead by the accidental explosion of an explosive walking stick, or American life preserver. A report of firearms was heard, and a moment afterwards the deceased was found dead on some steps leading from the back yard to the Mayor's residence, F. house, Manningham. It is supposed that as the deceased was ascending the steps the trigger was in some manner struck.

24 December 1884

FATAL ACCIDENT

A fatal accident occurred on Saturday evening to the Rev. Mr. Vaughan, of Tallarn, near Malpas, Cheshire. He got out of his carriage to speak to a man on the top of a load of corn. The man, approaching too near the edge of the load, fell over, and the prongs of a pitchfork he had in his hand struck Mr. Vaughan in the chest and penetrated his heart. He died in less than half an hour. Mrs. Vaughan was with her husband when the accident occurred.

31 August 1885

THROWING RICE AT WEDDINGS

The danger of the custom of throwing rice at weddings has just been exemplified. The vicar of St. James the Less,

Bethnal-green, has for many years solemnized the ceremony of marriage free to any who choose to avail themselves of his kindness. It is usual for the friends to wait outside and give the couples a reception with a shower of rice, and to such an extent has the practice grown that the neighbouring grocers keep parcels ready wrapped for the occasion. The brides are generally protected by their veils, the bridegrooms are less fortunate, and yesterday one of them received several grains in his eyes. When he raised his arm to shield himself a fresh fusillade was opened upon him, and it was only when he staggered back in pain that it dawned upon his friends that they had given him a reception with more vigour than discretion. After a vain attempt to clear his eyes he was led to a surgery adjacent, and he will now have to pass in the ward of a hospital what would have been his honeymoon. It appears that this is not by any means the first serious accident caused in this way.

26 May 1886

SINGULAR DEATH

For some time past the owner of a bear which has been performing at the Belmont Music-hall, Mile-end, has offered to give 10s. to any person successfully throwing the animal in a wrestling match. On Saturday night Jack Picton, the professional boxer, a very heavy man, weighing 16 st. 8 lb., took up the challenge, but instead of his throwing the bear the animal threw him, inflicting such injuries that he died in the London Hospital yesterday morning.

31 December 1890

SINGULAR INCIDENT IN COURT

A barrister had just finished making an application to the Master of the Rolls yesterday, when the back of his gown was observed to be smouldering. On the gown being hastily removed, a dense volume of smoke burst forth, and it became evident that a serious conflagration was proceeding in the learned gentleman's coat tails. After apologizing to the Bench, the learned counsel was compelled to divest himself of his coat, and hurried out of Court in his shirt sleeves.

22 July 1886

REX v GOLDSTEIN (TAILORS TO THE LAW) ADJOURNED TILL TUESDAY!

TWO MEN POISONED

A case of poisoning occurred at Old Park Farm, Margam, near Swansea, on Tuesday evening. About half-past seven a young man employed by Mr. W. S. Powell, J.P., went over to Old Park Farm to pay a visit to a man named Hussey, who has for some time past filled the post of head bailiff to Miss Styles, of Bridgend. Whilst the visitor was there Hussey requested a boy in his service to get a jar of beer. The boy did as requested, but instead of bringing beer he brought a jar containing a liquid for sheep dipping. The young man took a mouthful and said it had a queer taste. Hussey asked for the jar, and, placing it to his mouth, took a good draught. It was found that both Hussey and the young man had been poisoned. Medical assistance was speedily called in, and Dr. Davies, of Taibach, did all that he could, but it was of no avail. Both men died, after suffering great pain, at 3 o'clock yesterday morning.

2 January 1890

The horrible . . .

ACCIDENT WITH A HAIR-PIN

The following extraordinary accident occurred last week at the Versailles theatre during the performance of the "Sonneur de Saint Paul". The actor who took the principal part being on the stage with a young actress who wore in her head-dress a long pin in the Italian fashion, in the energy of his action inadvertently knocked the pin from her hair, and drove it with much violence into the eye of the prompter, who uttered a piercing shriek, and fell senseless with the pain. On examination it was found that the organs of sight were not injured, the pin having entered the corner of the eye, and there is every hope that no serious consequences will ensue.

19 April 1839

SINGULAR ACCIDENT

Yesterday morning a singular accident occurred to a man named Charles Benjamin, 26 years of age, who resides at No. 3, Lambeth-street, Whitechapel. It appears that he was walking along the Whitechapel-road with a pipe in his mouth when he struck against a post, by which the pipe was forced into his throat, and a portion of it broken off. He fell down convulsed with agony. He was conveyed immediately to the London Hospital, where he remains in a very dangerous condition.

14 December 1841

FEARFUL SITUATION

A Mr. Gray, of Providence, painter of the Congregational meeting-house, in Kingston, Rhode Island, last week ascended the steeple to take off the vane for gilding, and having left the ladders, climbed the iron spire to the distance of 12 or 13 feet above, relying upon the ball, half way up the spire, to rest his feet on, and from which position he could take the vane off with his right hand. While he was in the very act, the ball on which his feet rested gave way and ran down the spire. At this moment he was raising the vane over the end of it; as he did so, the spire growing smaller, made a convenient place for his thumb to keep the balancer in the gudgeon bore, when the ball gave way under him and sank. The vane falling back with his thumb in the gudgeon bore, held him fast, with his feet dangling in the air. He remained in this perilous situation until a man ascended the spire, and placing his shoulder under his feet, at once relieved him. The scene was terrible to behold. (*American paper*)

14 August 1846

DREADFUL ACCIDENT AT BRUGES

A fearful accident happened on Friday last at the Madeleine church, Bruges. One of the priests, while performing mass, was suddenly struck to the ground by the falling on his forehead of the marble head of an infant Jesus, which had become detached from its body. Fracture of the skull and a severe wound were the consequence to the unhappy clergyman, who, after lingering in great agony, died yesterday. (*Bruges John Bull*)

3 May 1847

87

SINGULAR ACCIDENT

A labouring man named John Hacker, in the employ of Mr. Bayley, of Hempstead, near this city, a few days ago very nearly acted the part of his own executioner, by inflicting upon himself the very aristocratic punishment of beheading. He was lopping a tree, and was standing upon one branch, while he was cutting away one above him. In this position the lower branch broke off, and the poor fellow let go his axe and came tumbling to the ground, the weapon following him, and falling upon the back of his neck inflicted what at first had the appearance of a very dangerous wound, but which happily turned out to be far less serious than was at first apprehended. The cut was about three inches in length, and caused a good deal of blood to flow, but it was not deep, and none of the more important arteries were severed. The sufferer is now out of all danger, but he was considerably alarmed, and gave indication of his dislike of the distinguished mode of death which had so well nigh befallen him; perhaps he was aware that the cutting off of heads was formerly an aristocratic privilege, and his modesty would not allow him willingly to invade this valuable prerogative of his betters. *(Gloucester paper)*

21 December 1842

EXTRAORDINARY OCCURRENCE

On Friday last, shortly after daylight, two men, living at Sedlesham, near Bognor, Sussex, were engaged in netting small fish for bait. One of them named Jeffreys, having caught some small soles, was, according to custom, about to lay hold of one with his teeth, in order to draw it through the mesh, when it made a sudden effort to free itself from his grasp, and darted through the mouth into the larynx, with its head in the gullet. The fins being extended transfixed it in that situation. The man became totally overpowered, and the attempts of his companion to withdraw it were unavailing. Medical aid was sent for (a distance of four miles) but when the medical man arrived he found life totally extinct, and declined operating to remove the fish, judging it necessary not to interfere before an inspection had been made by the coroner and jury. The breadth of the fish was about three fingers, and it continued to flicker for many hours. This ill-fated individual was a young man, and has left a wife and three children to deplore his loss. A small subscription has been raised at Bognor for the widow, and it is hoped that the humane will forward to her donations, which may be conveniently effected by enclosing postage stamps.

27 August 1847

HORRIBLE DEATH

Yesterday (Friday) Mr. Baker, the Coroner for East Middlesex, received information of the following extraordinary and horrible death of a person named Mitchell, a dairyman, of Shoulder of Mutton-lane, near the North Country Pink, Limehouse. It appears that on Thursday morning, about 4 o'clock, the deceased got up as was his usual custom and went to milk the cows; nothing more was seen or heard of him till 7 o'clock, when some men perceived a portion of a blue apron projecting through the top of a pile of cowdung in the yard. Upon making a closer inspection they found that it was the deceased's apron and that the body was immersed head first in the soil. With all possible expedition the deceased was got out, but life was quite extinct and had been so for some time. It is supposed that the unfortunate man was walking along the edge of the shoot, and that he overbalanced himself and fell head foremost into the soil. An inquest will be held on the body this day (Saturday).

4 November 1848

STRANGE CIRCUMSTANCE

A boy named Edwin Hayball, of Chard parish, one day last week fell into a millpond, and was supposed to be drowned; he was, however, taken out of the water and the body carried home. Everybody believed the child dead except his mother, whose affliction was very great. She took him in her arms and held him before the fire. After nearly half an hour the child showed symptoms of returning consciousness, upon which some change in the position of the body took place, when it was discovered that the child's foot had been in the fire and was dreadfully burnt. A surgeon having been called in did what was necessary, and the child was getting on very well. About three days after the mother placed him before the fire for a moment whilst she went into the garden, and on her return she was horror-struck to find her child burnt almost to a cinder. It is a singular coincidence that a girl, the cousin of the above-named Edwin Hayball, a short time since fell into the fire, and one of her breasts was almost entirely consumed; in her agony she ran to the millpond, to allay the pain by bathing the breast with cold water, when she fell in and was drowned. An inquest has been held on Edwin Hayball, and a verdict of "Accidental death" returned. (*Devon Chronicle*)
30 November 1848

HORRIBLE ACCIDENT

As an omnibus was on Wednesday passing along the Place de la Bastille volumes of smoke suddenly issued from it, and the passengers were observed to descend in terrible confusion. In the interior was a man who was rolling about in terrible suffering. This man, it appeared, had imprudently placed a bottle of nitric acid in his coat pocket, and a jolt of the vehicle caused the bottle to break. The liquid spread over him, and occasioned the smoke. In a moment his clothes were reduced to cinders, and his flesh was horribly burnt. A lady seated

91

92

next to him had her silk gown entirely destroyed, and she was besides slightly injured. One person had a bundle of chymical matches, which caught fire. The flames extended to the vehicle and did it considerable damage. When the passengers had descended, the man who had the nitric acid was conveyed to the Hospital St. Antoine. He was in an alarming state, and his flesh fell from him. *(Galignani's Messenger)*

26 July 1851

CURIOUS ACCIDENT

On Monday last an accident of a singular but distressing nature happened to one of our townsmen. A pair of fanners* were being conveyed in a cart along the road to the Whins, when, from some cause or other, the horse ran off. Mr. Drummond, millwright, the person who has met with the accident, at first stepped forward to stop the horse, but, fearing danger, started hastily back. Behind Mr. Drummond was a lad bearing an axe upon his shoulder. Upon the sharp edge of the instrument Mr. Drummond unfortunately ran, and the consequence was that his nose was very nearly cut off. So complete was the cut the nose fell over upon the mouth, and was suspended by the slightest portion of the integument. Mr. Drummond instantly applied his handkerchief to his face, and proceeded to Dr. Brotherston, who was fortunately in his own house at the moment. As may be supposed, the sight was a hideous one, the accident presenting an insight into the interior of the face. We are happy to say that, under Dr. Brotherston's judicious treatment, the nose has been replaced, and there is every hope of the cure being so effectual that scarcely any trace of the accident will by and by be visible. *(Alloa Advertiser)*

18 December 1855

* A device for separating corn from chaff.

APPALLING DEATH

Considerable excitement was caused in the town of Lewes on Thursday morning by a rumour that a young man named Matthew Gladman had met with his death by falling into the soil of a watercloset, the evening before, on the premises of Dr. Smythe, High Street. It turned out to be too true. It appears that the young fellow incautiously went out to the watercloset in the dark. He found that the door was fastened with a rope, the boards having been taken up preparatory to the cess-pit in connexion with the closet being cleaned out. That rope he appears to have untied, and to have tumbled at once into the soil below. The body, on being extricated, was wiped dry, and galvanism applied, but in vain. It is the opinion of the medical attendant that asphyxia by the sulphuretted hydrogen gas caused instantaneous death.

1 March 1856

HEROIC WALK

Blondin, the tight-rope dancer, has narrowly escaped death. He was crossing a tight-rope in Ohio after dusk, wheeling a barrow, and encircled with a blaze of fireworks – doubtless in jealous imitation of the late splendid meteor.* Before he had reached the middle of his aerial route, one of the pieces exploded and set fire to his clothing. There was no time to halt and extinguish the flames, and the modern Phaeton could only keep on his course and suffer the torture of being slowly blistered. With heroic self-control he gained the end of his journey and succeeded in smothering the fire, but not until he was sadly burnt.

1 September 1860

---

* This was a spectacular meteor seen in New York and other American cities on 20 July 1860.

FIRE BLANKET

AT LEAST THE ROPE'S OK!

AMENITIES OF THE CANADIAN CLIMATE

One morning a little fellow about 8 years old, a son of Mr. Gillan, bookseller, while playing with some other boys in North street, approached a lamppost, and carelessly applied his tongue to the gray frosted surface, when in an instant, to the boy's own horror and the utter astonishment of his playmates, he was held fast by his tongue to the post, suffering very severe pain, and wholly unable to help or extricate himself. Of course the boy could not speak, and could only manifest his feelings by signs with his hands. Various applications of warm tea, steam etc. were made by some neighbours, who heard the unusual noise made by the other boys and came to learn what was the matter, but of no avail; such was the action of the cold iron that the hold was even getting tighter. After about 10 minutes had elapsed the boy's father heard of the affair, and, hastening to his relief, he took a knife and was obliged to cut the tongue loose, leaving its skin still fast to the post and causing the blood to flow very profusely. Immediately on his release the poor little fellow became insensible and was taken home. (*A Canadian paper*)

29 December 1858

A NEW SENSATION

The frequenters of music-halls and other places of entertainment, where the attractions are heightened by performances on the tight-rope or flying trapeze, which give every visitor the chance of witnessing a fatal accident, would have envied the inhabitants of Middletown, in Missouri, had they known the thrilling scene which occurred there on the morning of the 12th of May. The 'Middletown Banner' says:— "The little village was thrown into a fearful fever of excitement on that day by an awful catastrophe which occurred to the band lately attached to James Robinson and Co.'s Circus and Animal Show, and led by Professor M. C. Sexton. The management had determined to produce something novel in the way of a band chariot, and conceived the idea of mounting the band upon the colossal den of performing Numidian lions. Although repeatedly warned by Professor Sexton that he deemed the cage insecure and dangerous in the extreme, the managers still compelled the band to sit upon it. As the driver endeavoured to take a turn in the streets, on the morning of the accident, the leaders became entangled, and threw the entire team into confusion, and ended by starting off at a gallop. The fore wheel of the cage came into contact with a large rock with such force as to cause the braces and stanchions which supported the roof to give way, thereby precipitating the band into the awful pit below. For an instant the crowd were paralyzed with fear, but for a moment only, and then arose such a shriek of agony as was never heard before. The groans of terror from the poor victims who were being torn to pieces by the lions below were heartrending and sickening to the last degree. Some few of the bandsmen managed to climb over the sides of the cage, and then fell senseless to the ground, while the others were seen struggling with the wild beasts in a mass of hideous confusion. A hardware store which happened to stand opposite was invaded, and pitchforks, crowbars, and long bars of iron – in fact, every available weapon – was brought into requisition. The side doors of the cage were quickly torn from their fastenings, and then a horrible sight was presented to view. Mingled with the brilliant uniform of the poor unfortunates lay legs and arms torn from their sockets and half devoured, while the savage brutes glared ferociously with their sickly green-coloured eyes upon the crowd. At this moment Professor Charles White arrived and gave orders with regard to extricating the dead and wounded. Stationing men with forks and bars at every available point, he sprang fearlessly into the den and commenced raising the dead and wounded, whom he passed to the people outside. He had removed the last wounded man, and was proceeding to gather up the remains of the lifeless, when the 'Mammoth lion', known

97

by the name of Old Nero, sprang, with a frightful roar, upon him, fastening his teeth and claws in his neck and shoulders and lacerating him in a horrible manner. Professor White made three efforts to shake the monster off, but without avail, and then gave orders to fire upon him. The contents of four of Colt's navys* were immediately poured into the carcass of the lion, who fell dead with a savage howl, and the brave little man, notwithstanding the fearful manner in which he was wounded, never left the cage until every vestige of the dead was carefully gathered together and placed upon a sheet. It was found that three of the 10 bandsmen were killed outright and four others terribly lacerated. The names of the killed are August Schoer, Conrad Freeiz, and Charles Greiner. Coffins were procured, and an immediate burial determined upon, as the bodies were so torn as to be unrecognizable to their most intimate friends." *(Pall Mall Gazette)*

7 July 1870

AFTER EDGAR POE

The 'Nord' is responsible for the following account of a horrible accident which has just happened at Montrouge. A M. Dumas, residing there, an agent of manufacturing chymists in Rouen, has kept for the last three months a black ape, which had been brought to him from Africa. It was M. Dumas' custom every evening before going to bed to take a glass of 'eau sucrée', into which he put a little orange water. The monkey, which was in the bedroom and saw him do this, is believed to have formed the purpose of repeating the act. M. Dumas had just received from his employers a specimen of nitric acid which he was to sell to a retail dealer in Paris. After having opened and examined the contents of the bottle, he prepared his glass of sugar and water, went to bed, and fell asleep. The monkey then poured the contents of the bottle

---

* A type of revolver invented by Samuel Colt (1814-62).

into the glass and retired. Feeling thirsty during the night, M. Dumas rose and swallowed the poison. He died shortly afterwards, having suffered the most excruciating agony. The 'Siècle' adds to what is stated above, that when the neighbours came in, the monkey was seen with the empty bottle in its hands.

2 October 1872

TO THE EDITOR OF THE TIMES

Sir,— I have seen two short statements about the sad death of Captain Berry, but as I suppose that the account I had from my son is the only authentic one that can have reached this country, I send it to you as I have it from him.

His letter is dated "Maipopo's, near North end of Nyassa, 17th Dec., 1883. But now I have a fearfully sad story to tell. Two hunters came up from Natal to shoot, one Lieutenant Crawshay, who has had fever ever since his arrival and has never been out, and Captain Berry, who has been about with us for eight or ten days. Well, last Thursday we were upon the Kawni river, had had a long, unsuccessful tramp after elephants the day before, and about 8 a.m. we went down to the river to bathe as usual. Berry, Munro, and I went in and Pulley came down a little later. I was just leaving the water, Munro and Berry still in, when something appeared to go wrong, and Berry's head went under water. In a few seconds he rose further out, struggling. He was pulled under at once and he next came up in deep water near the other side, an immense alligator having him right across the body. He seemed then insensible and utterly at the brute's mercy. As, before we knew anything was wrong, the great brute's tail was towards us and it was off into deep water, we were powerless to help. It was two minutes before we could get a rifle down, and by that time it was too late, and so our companion was seized and carried off within three or four yards of us, and just where we had been bathing a few minutes

100

before. We watched the banks all the way down the river to a fish weir and shot five alligators during the day – one, 13ft. long, close to where Berry was taken, and truly with such a brute a man had no chance. As yet no remains of the body have been found. It is fearfully sad; the first time a white man has been taken in that way as far as we know." On the 23rd of December he adds:— "Not a trace found of poor Berry's body. "Be ye therefore ready also", &c., is plainly written here." . . .

I am, Sir, your obedient servant,
John Moir
52 Castle-street, Edinburgh.

5 May 1884

SUFFOCATED BY LOCUSTS

A horrible and striking proof of the seriousness of the locust plague in Algiers has just reached Paris in the news of the death, at the Douar of Sidi-Eral, of M. Kunckel d'Herculais, a French naturalist, who was in Algiers on a mission to discover some means of destroying the locust eggs, and who has been suffocated, almost as if through the vengeance of these insects. On May 17 the heat was so excessive that M. Kunckel sought shelter in the shade of some bushes of a shrubbery. He was overtaken by an enormous cloud of locusts, in which he was absolutely submerged, and he apparently struggled in vain to release himself, endeavouring to set fire to the shrubbery. When he was discovered at about 3 o'clock in the afternoon by some Arabs his beard, hair and cravat had been eaten away.

19 May 1891

Serves you right! . .

A WOMAN STRANGLED BY HER
BONNET-STRINGS

An extremely dissipated, drunken, and disorderly woman of
the name of Elizabeth Kenchen met her death on Wednesday
night last in the following novel manner. She had been all the
day luxuriating in her accustomed manner – namely, drinking quarterns of gin, in the performance of which no woman
in Westminster surpassed her. She went to bed intoxicated,
and yesterday morning she was found absolutely hanged in
her own bonnet-strings. It appears that she went to bed with
her bonnet on, but in that restlessness which intoxication
creates she fell out of bed, and her bonnet becoming fastened
between the bedstead or bedpost and the wall, she was so
drunk as not to be able to unloose the strings, and was, in
consequence, strangled.

28 June 1839

WOMAN'S FALL

An extraordinary case of the consequence of female curiosity
occurred at Uffington, near Stamford, on Friday last, very
early in the morning. A married woman, about 35 years of
age, the wife of a labourer named Stanton, was indulging in
very attentive observation of the proceedings in a neighbouring house, when, leaning too far out of a window, in her
earnestness to see all that could be seen, she lost her hold, and
was precipitated heavily to the ground, from a height of
about 15 feet. Her fall being upon a hard pavement, she
fractured her right collar-bone, three or four of her ribs, her

breast-bone, and her left arm, besides dreadfully bruising herself in other parts of the body. The poor woman was brought to the Stamford Infirmary, where she now lies in a precarious state. (*Stamford Mercury*)

6 April 1840

DEATH OF A REPUBLICAN

A letter from Geneva states:— "On the 31st ult., several communes of Soleure held a grand festival in commemoration of the anniversary of the adoption of the Bernese constitution. The provisions for the feast were taken to the summit of a mountain. An immense bonfire was made in the evening, which, however, occasioned a lamentable accident. As the flames began to subside, a blacksmith, named Girard, remarkable for his violent radicalism, raised one of the brands which had fallen from the heap, and kicked it with his foot into the fire, exclaiming, "So would I have every aristocrat served!" In doing this his foot slipped, and he fell back over a precipice of 300 feet deep. He was killed on the spot, leaving a widow with three children, and a fourth in expectancy, whom the aristocrats he reviled will have to maintain." (*Galignani's Messenger*)

23 August 1841

AWFUL VISITATION

On Sunday night last Nottingham and its vicinity was visited by one of the most extraordinary storms which have happened for a considerable number of years past. The weather during the day had been, on the whole, very fine; and there was a total absence of that oppressive closeness which is usually the precursor of thunder. At a little before sunset

103

104

there was scarcely a cloud to be seen, but shortly afterwards a dense mass gathered near the south-western horizon, and flashes of sheet-lightning streamed forth in quick succession. As the darkness advanced, these electric discharges followed each other still more rapidly, until at length the heavens from the north to the south were completely illumined as with fire-works. At about 10 o'clock it commenced raining; and the shower, which lasted till nearly 11, was one of the most heavy known for a long period . . . But the most awful occurrence took place at the Milton's Head Inn, on the Derby-road. A man named Alfred Greenwood, of Radford, a lace-maker, who was drinking there, was using some of the most disgustingly blasphemous language conceivable. Amongst other things, he said that he wished a thunderbolt would fall through the roof, and kill everybody in the house. One of the bystanders rebuked him for his impious wish, and he replied, "I don't care: I fear neither God nor devil." When he had spoken these shocking words he sat down, and remained about ten minutes with his eyes steadily fixed upon the ceiling, and appeared like one greatly amazed; he then gradually reeled, and fell into the arms of a soldier who was sitting against him. He was struck blind! His eyes were then firmly closed, but in seven or eight minutes he opened them for about a quarter of a minute, when they closed again, and he ejaculated, "The Lord forgive me;" to which every one in the room, about 20 in number, responded "Amen". A surgeon was instantly fetched, who bled him and administered other remedies; but the unhappy man appeared nearly frantic. He was soon after removed home, and since then to the General Hospital, where he has received the unremitting attention of the first medical practitioners in the town. We understand that he has since been enabled to see a little, and that hopes are entertained that his sight will be ultimately restored to him.

9 July 1845

A CAREFUL WOMAN

On Monday afternoon, as the passengers who had just landed from one of the steam-boats on the south side of the Tay Ferry were making their way along the pier, a smart shower of rain fell, whereupon an elderly lady, more careful for her bonnet than cautious about her person, drew her dress over her head, and having thus effectually protected that piece of millinery from the falling rain, forgot that she had also as effectually obscured the line of vision; and striking off at a tangent (in mistake, of course), walked into the harbour, the tide being within two hours from high water. She was got safely out.

9 November 1860

RECKLESS BATHERS

A somewhat singular occurrence took place at Tynemouth on Wednesday last. It appears that a young lady, the daughter of a medical gentleman, entered one of the numerous bathing machines on the Long Sands. The young lady, on entering the machine, was duly cautioned by the owner, and also on her alighting in the sea, of the risk she would necessarily run by venturing too far out, at that particular state of the tide and sea. Nothing daunted, however, she rushed heedlessly on, regardless of the shouts of her adviser, who, at length, when he found that persuasive measures were quite unavailing, mounted a horse, whip in hand, and rode to her rescue, threatening at the same time, to apply it to the lady's shoulders should she still persist in risking her life in the manner above stated, on which she hastily returned to the machine to dress, on making her exit from which she intimated that it would certainly be the last time she would patronize his bathing machines. Although so recently as Sunday last Mr. Falconer lost his life on the same sands, and his body has not yet been recovered, nothing will deter some people. The owner of the machine certainly had not recourse to the most refined measures by which to deter the fair bather; but there can be little doubt that her parents and relations would have infinitely preferred her having received a sound whipping rather than have heard of her death by drowning owing to her own folly and indiscretion.

6 September 1864

ATTACK UPON A MAN BY AN ELEPHANT

On Monday, as Edmonds' (late Wombwell's) menagerie was entering Maidstone for the fair, which commenced yesterday, a serious occurrence happened. A fine elephant, with some camels, was drawing the first caravan, when the procession halted for the purpose of ascertaining the correct route. A boy in the crowd offered the elephant an apple, when one of the men in attendance interfered. The animal, which had for some time shown symptoms of anger towards this man, became irritated, and seized him with his trunk around the waist, dashed him to the ground, and endeavoured to gore him with his tusks. The man, however, succeeded in crawling away, when the animal again seized him with his trunk and dashed him against the wall. The poor fellow was at last rescued by the crowd, and was found to be severely injured. Several of his ribs were broken, an arm and a leg were fractured, and he was bruised in several places. A shutter was obtained, and he was conveyed to the West Kent General Hospital, where he now lies in a very precarious condition. The man is an itinerant exhibitor of a show, named Charles Nixon, of Derby. He is about 40 years of age, and is only an occasional helper of those employed with the menagerie. The keeper, who was riding on the back of the elephant, did all in his power to divert the attention of the enraged animal, which in general is as quiet and docile as a child. The injured man, it is said, once teased the animal in a show in a manner which it never forgot.

18 October 1865

SWALLOWING PINS

The danger of making a pin repository of the mouth has just been exemplified at Penzance. A Mrs. Rawlings was engaged in a garden hanging out some clothes, and with a view to save time she placed a number of pins in her mouth. Being startled by an urgent request to go into the house to her child, she turned round very suddenly, and while so doing 17 pins slipped down her throat, most of them lodging in her gullet. The poor woman suffered fearful pain. A neighbour resorted to the old-fashioned, and in this case efficacious, method of persistently slapping the patient's back. In the course of a couple of hours 14 pins were slapped up and three down, and beyond the pain and irritation of the throat no harm has been done.

14 November 1866

DANCING IN SPURS

A singular accident is reported from Dublin. Colonel Wardlaw was dancing at one of the Viceregal entertainments when his spur caught in a lady's gown, and he was thrown down with such violence that he fractured his hip. May we ask, in the name of common sense, what is the use of spurs in a ballroom? Is the exhibition of these dangerous weapons due to the theory that officers should be ready for action at a moment's notice? Are their horses kept ready saddled at the door? or do they sleep in their spurs? Possibly it may be the custom to wear them in the presence of ladies from the effect produced by the clank and clatter of swords and spurs. We have heard of half-sovereigns being substituted for rowels, in order to improve the tone of the ring. But could not a similar effect be produced by a bell hung round the neck? At any rate it would not be as dangerous as the wearing of spurs on the heels has proved itself to be. *(Pall Mall Gazette)*

26 February 1870

BEATING A HORSE WITH A GUN

On Wednesday afternoon last Dr. Guy, the coroner for the Doncaster district of West Riding, held an inquest at Awkley, a village three miles to the south of Doncaster, to inquire into the cause of the death of John Wastnedge, aged 18 years, who met with injuries which resulted in his death from beating a horse with a loaded gun. The deceased had a loaded gun in his possession a day or two ago, and was close to Hampole-wood when he noticed a fellow servant ploughing in a field. He went up and appears to have assisted to attach a third horse to the plough. To start it he struck it with the stock end of the gun, and in doing so the gun went off and the contents struck his right arm, shattered it very much, and at the same time set fire to his clothes. Firth, the servant who was ploughing, at once removed him to the house of his master, Mr. Littlewood, of Hampole, and subsequently he was removed to his father's house at Awkley, where he died. The jury returned a verdict that the deceased met with his death from injuries caused by a gunshot wound. The Coroner at the close of the inquiry made some pertinent remarks upon the fatal cases that have recently occurred in Yorkshire from the incautious use of firearms.

16 November 1866

Narrow escapes . . .

MARVELLOUS

Extract of a letter from Armagh, dated January 3:— A labouring man named Patrick Woods, in the employment of Messrs. Harrington, lived with a family of six young children, in a house in Chapel-lane, the roof of which fell in, with a tremendous crash, between five and six o'clock on the aforementioned morning. The man, who is of religious habits, and bears a good character, states that for three or four nights previous to the accident he got little sleep, and when he did fall asleep he soon woke from turbulent dreams; that on the night of Tuesday, he felt his fears increased on going to bed, and in the course of it he became so much agitated that he got up, dressed himself, raised his wife and children, and helping on the clothes of the younger, and hurrying the older ones, forced them out of the house; on turning back a few paces to close the door, which he had neglected to do on leaving it, and while he held the latch in his hand, he heard the timber giving way, and in a moment the whole roof fell in with a frightful crash! On examining the place at day-light, the walls only remained standing: the roof had fallen so completely in, that had it not pleased the All-bountiful to warn the man of the calamity, every soul in the cabin would have been killed by the collision, and buried in the ruins. To strengthen the certainty of this marvellous affair, and to render the account of it more awfully imposing, it is proper to mention, that the house underwent a thorough repair a very short time before; and, judging from appearance, either inside or out, no one could have had the most distant apprehension of the occurrence. The man himself says he had no cause whatever to expect the like, and attributes their deliverance to God alone. *(Newry Telegraph)*
15 January 1829

A PINPRICK

On Monday, a boy 14 years of age entered a travelling exhibition of wild beasts in Drummond-street, Euston-square, and incautiously pricked the trunk of an elephant with a pin; the huge animal, irritated at the proceeding, coiled its trunk round the body of the youth, and lifting him from the ground, was about to dash him against the side of the caravan, when the keeper called out loudly, which caused the elephant to let go its hold, and the affrighted little fellow was fortunately dropped down unhurt. Had not the keeper been present at the moment, the probability is that the boy's life would have been sacrificed.

27 May 1841

FALL OF A CHIMNEY-POT

On Saturday morning the following miraculous escape occurred in the New-cut, Lambeth. A little boy named Frank Holmes, only seven years of age, in the employ of Mr. Ballard, chimney-sweeper, Lower-marsh, Lambeth, ascended a chimney in the house of a person residing in the New-cut, for the purpose of cleaning it. On reaching the top, on which was a chimney-pot, he rattled his brush, and when in the act of doing so, the pot became loosened from the mortar, and with the little fellow in it fell off the chimney, and rolling down the tiles, bounded off into the street, a height of between 40 and 50 feet. The bystanders who witnessed the occurrence ran to him, expecting he was killed on the spot but were astonished to find he had escaped with only a few bruises and the loss of three of his teeth. This affords another instance of the necessity of legislative inter-ference on behalf of this suffering class of children. An act of Parliament abolishing the employment of climbing-boys will come into operation in July, 1842, when all boys who are not out of their apprenticeship may be transferred to a master of

113

some other trade, or have their indentures cancelled by a magistrate in petty sessions.

9 August 1841

SAVED BY CRUSHING

A few days ago a little boy belonging to one of the farm servants at East Leys, got upon the frame of a large metal roller while it was at work, but a sudden jerk of the machine threw him right over and immediately in front of it, and, before the horses could be stopped, the roller had gone completely over him, but, to the astonishment of the driver, who expected to find a lifeless corpse, he was taken up very little hurt, the weight of the machine having bedded him a considerable way into the ground, and this it was which, under God, saved him. (*The Witness*)

23 September 1841

AN ESCAPE

On Monday night Richard Allen, one of the Duke of Buckingham's Wotton Underwood gamekeepers, had a providential escape from death. He was on duty at Risdalpark Farm, Brill, and observed a person searching about as if for game; it was dusk, and he laid himself down in a furrow to watch the man's movements; while there a man shot at him, wounded him, and he became insensible. The person who shot at him was a labourer named Coggins, in the employ of Mr. Bond. His version of the affair is as follows:— "I was sent by my master to try to shoot a rabbit; while in search of it I saw something black, which I took to be a rabbit, at about 30 yards distance. I fired my gun; on my going up to it I found it to be Allen, he was stunned; on coming to himself he said he was shot. What I took to be the rabbit was Allen's black cap." The cap was blown from the man's head some yards, and perforated with shot; a few only entered his person.

14 October 1842

ACCIDENT TO GENERAL TOM THUMB

"General Tom Thumb"* was taking a drive near Clifton on Sunday afternoon, in an open carriage, accompanied by his father, his guardian, and his preceptor, Mr. Sherman. The General and the latter were on the driver's box, and on descending a steep hill, the horse took fright, ran at the top of his speed, and dashed against a high stone wall with such force as to break his neck, and shiver the shafts and a portion of the carriage to atoms. The two inside gentlemen escaped with a few slight bruises. Mr. Sherman had seen the approaching danger, and held the General firmly in his arms, and the moment the concussion occurred he cleared the horse and wall, the latter nearly 9 feet in height, and landed safely in the adjoining field, preserving his charge harmless! (*Globe*)

21 August 1844

WONDERFUL PRESERVATION

A young woman named Mary Webster, who resides with her widowed mother, near Mr. Simmon's paperworks, in the Via Gellia, at Bonsall has recently had the narrowest escape from a miserable death that we ever remember to have heard of under anything like similar circumstances. The young woman, who is 22 years of age, stout, and rather good-look-

* American midget circus performer (1838–83).

115

ing, is unfortunately of somewhat weak intellect. It happens that shortly previous to Tuesday week she was walking with her mother on a foot-road leading from Bonsall to Ible, when, at a place called Bonsall Lees, a common cotton handkerchief which she wore was blown off by the wind, it being rather rough at the time, and before it could be recovered it went down the shaft of a deserted lead mine which had been carelessly left unsecured. The loss of the handkerchief seems to have affected her in an extraordinary degree, and on the night of Tuesday week, about 10 o'clock, she left her home, and although diligent enquiries were made after her, nothing was ascertained respecting her until the following Monday morning. On that morning her mother, who was then seeking her, inquired of a miner, named John Massey, who was working on Bonsall Lees, if he knew anything of her daughter, and received for answer that he did not. The distracted mother went forward on her now almost hopeless search, and being in the neighbourhood of the shaft into which the handkerchief had blown, she went to it, and shouted down, when, strange to say, her ears were greeted with the voice of her lost daughter, who, at the expiration of a week's entombment without sustenance of any kind, appeared to recognize the voice of her parent. The overjoyed mother now hastened back to Massey (the miner to whom she had last spoken), and he lost no time in obtaining the assistance of some brother miners, who speedily collected the necessary tackling for rescuing the miserable sufferer from her living grave, and everything being adjusted to secure as far as possible the safety of the object of their humane exertions, Massey and another miner, William Bunting, descended the shaft, which is 20 yards deep, and perpendicular, and found her in a crouching position at the shaft foot, sensible, but nearly bereft of physical strength, and to use Massey's words, "as cold as a corpse." She had (no doubt in moments of delirium) unclothed herself to the waist downwards, and taken off her shoes and one stocking, and she had actually recovered the lost handkerchief, which was lying beside her, and in which was tied up one of her shoes. Having been safely attached to the rope, she was drawn to the

116

surface, and during her ascent she attempted to hold on, but was, of course, too far exhausted to do so effectually. Perhaps the strangest circumstance connected with this strange tale is, that a few minutes after arriving at the surface, she told her mother that before she attempted to descend the shaft in search of the handkerchief, she had taken off her gown, and hidden it in a wall, the gown was found exactly as described by her. She was now carefully removed home, and on putting her to bed it was found that she had received no external injury beyond comparatively slight lacerations and bruises. Weak restoratives were sparingly administered, and under the care of Mr. Evans, surgeon, of Winster, there is every likelihood of her restoration to perfect health. She states that she believed the shaft was only two or three yards deep, as she looked into it on the day she lost her handkerchief, and thought she saw the bottom. She had descended apparently four or five feet, when a peg which bore her weight, proving rotten, broke, and she was precipitated, as already described, nearly 20 yards to the bottom, her fall being, no doubt, in some degree broken by the resistance of air against her clothes. She complains of having suffered horribly from thirst, and had eaten part of her under garments, but does not seem to possess any knowledge of her own as to the length of time her living entombment had endured. (*Nottingham Journal*)

14 September 1844

NARROW ESCAPE

On Wednesday last a carriage and pair, containing three ladies, was waiting at the railway station at Rugby whilst the coachman went to make inquiries after some luggage. During his absence the horses, alarmed at the noise of the numerous engines that are constantly passing backwards and forwards at this point, turned round and started off at a rapid rate towards the town. A man engaged in mending the road,

alarmed at the approach of the carriage, removed his barrow, but dared not attempt to stop the horses; a young man, however, who lives at the Crown, seeing the dangerous position in which the ladies were placed, gallantly ran towards the horses, and succeeded in obtaining possession of the reins, and also in checking the progress of the spirited animals, after being dragged a distance of nearly 30 yards. It was almost miraculous that the parties in the carriage escaped without injury, as the road along which the horses ran is nearly at all times thronged with carriages of different descriptions passing to and from the station and the town. The ladies in the carriage, to show the estimation in which they held the courageous conduct of the young man by whose intervention their lives were most probably saved, presented him with the munificent sum of sixpence!

24 April 1847

118

SINGULAR ESCAPE FROM DROWNING

On Saturday week a man named Freeman, being at Lydbrook, paid a visit to Monmouth with a friend, and it was late at night before they separated, when each took a different route home. Freeman never having visited Monmouth before, took the wrong turning in the road; when he reached the turnpike, on the Dixton-road, being surcharged and fond of "heavy wet", he walked into the river, which, flowing rapidly from the late extensive rains, proved rather too powerful for the weak and tottering condition of Freeman's frame. The most extraordinary and singular part of the affair is his escape. There were some poachers carrying on their nocturnal depredations in the river, and hearing a splash, and rejoicing at the sound, thinking it was some fine salmon wagging his tail, they immediately spread and threw out their net, when, after considerable exertion in hauling and sundry givings away in the net, they beheld to their great surprise that they were the fishers of a man, possessing warmth and vitality. He was speedily removed by them to Monmouth, and soon recovered. This circumstance must prove a lesson to Freeman, and it is hoped prevent his being again caught in such a net, by a Bacchanalian *draught*. (*Bristol Times*)

7 November 1848

MARVELLOUS ESCAPE FROM DEATH

One of the most wonderful escapes from impending death that was ever heard or read of occurred on Saturday the 28th ult., in the person of a workman employed in the erection of the High Level-bridge across the Tyne. On Saturday morning, shortly after 8 o'clock, John Smith, of Newcastle, a middle-aged shipwright, in the service of Messrs. Hawks, Crawshay, and Sons, was at work at the High Level-bridge, the floors of which are laid in shipbuilding fashion; he had occasion to pass from the permanent to the temporary bridge, at the south end of the first water arch, counting from Newcastle. A loose plank extended from the one bridge to the other as a roadway, and when he placed his foot upon it it canted over. The end upon which he stepped had been lying, probably, upon some loose gravel. He was looking westward at the time, but found himself suddenly turned eastward, and with his head down. His thought at the moment was – "I'm gone!" Immediately below was the projecting cornice of the stone pier at the lower roadway of the bridge, on which he must dash in his descent, and thence be precipitated into the Tyne, at a depth from the plank of 100 feet; but he was miraculously arrested in his downward course. A huge nail had been driven to the depth of an inch and a half into the end of a crossbearer, on which the temporary platform rests. It served no purpose, but had apparently been driven in from mere caprice. The projecting head was John Smith's guardian angel; it caught his fustian trousers by the leg, a little above the hem (if that be the right word), and he hung suspended, swinging to and fro in the wind, and gazing downward upon the cornice and the flood, which threatened him with a double death. Edward Ward, a painter, with Messrs. Cummins and Co., was the first to observe his situation, and running up, held him by the leg; but Smith told him that he must obtain further assistance, or he could do him no good. Ward then alarmed the other workmen – some of whom procured a ladder, by which they got up to their comrade from the lower bridge, and released him from his peril. (*Gateshead Observer*)

10 August 1849

A FORTUNATE ESCAPE

A porter of a house in the Rue St. Lazare having yesterday gone on the roof to clean out the gutter, lost his balance and fell over into the court. Fortunately for him, some clothes

were drying on a line, across which he fell, and, his fall having been thus broken, the linen coming under him and forming a kind of bed, he escaped without the slightest injury (*Galignani's Messenger*)

30 September 1850

ALARMING OCCURRENCE

Newport, Tuesday: Last evening an alarming accident occurred in this town which occasioned the most frightful apprehensions as to the safety of nearly four hundred men, women, and children.

The Latter-day Saints who form a very large proportion of the population in Wales, have been holding their "conference" here within the past few days. To this gathering have assembled many of the "elders" of the fraternity, some of whom have held rank as "prophets" on the banks of the Salt River. Great preparations were made to celebrate this conference on an extensive scale; and, among other means, it is said that promises had been held out, and believed in by the too-credulous Welsh people, that "miracles would be performed!"

Yesterday afternoon, a large building named the Sunderland-hall, in which the body had held their services for a long period past, was filled to overflowing by the members of the sect, and their families, who reside in Newport, together with considerable numbers of the people from the hills, the colliery, ironworks, etc.

It is supposed that about four hundred persons were here assembled, about to join in partaking of tea after one of the services of the day. Several Mormon elders had given out the blessing, and some hints were thrown out that even that day might witness some of the great and miraculous powers of the saints. Scarcely had tea been commenced, when, without a moment's warning, exactly one half of the lofty and heavy ceiling of the building fell with a sudden crash. For a moment all was blinding and suffocating dust and confusion, then succeeded the most appalling shrieks and the most terrifying clamour; and, amidst the din and horrible confusion that ensued, people rushed from all the surrounding houses, apprehending that some great calamity had occurred. Fearful screams were again heard bursting forth, presently the windows of the hall were dashed out, and the affrighted creatures within flung themselves through the broken sashes to the ground below; some were observed clinging with extreme tenacity to the window-frames and sills, apprehending death within, and fearful of mutilated limbs if they fell. The doors were burst open from without as well as the piles of people heaped upon one another inside permitted, and ingress being at length obtained, the sight that presented itself was enough to appal the stoutest heart – beams and rafters, whole patches of ceiling, amidst clouds of dust, lying upon scores of people; while the tea-tables, affording protection to many, were crowded below with numbers crying aloud for mercy, for protection, and for a miracle to save them. The upper end of the hall, where the elders had been seated, was unhurt – the ceiling above their heads was unbroken. Immediate exertions were made, and in the course of an hour the wretched creatures were all extricated from the ruins, and on a minute search being instituted, not one was found missing; and, what is still more remarkable, although the beams and rafters were heavy, and some, with huge pieces of entire ceiling, fell directly upon the tables, and others in a direction that appeared to insure inevitable death, not one single Mormon was injured, though it was intimated that two or three unbelievers, who had gone thither to revile and sneer at the true followers of Joe Smith, received slight injuries, which may serve their consciences as remembrancers.

When the party were all extricated another hall was obtained, and there the remainder of the evening was devoted to an ovation to the elders and the prophets who had wrought the anticipated miracle of causing a ceiling to fall upon the heads of the saints without injury.

The occurrence has occasioned a remarkable sensation in the town.

14 July 1852

A NARROW ESCAPE

Late last night a man was discovered in a boat in the rapids, near the brink of the Falls of Niagara. The boat stuck fast on a rock, and was still there at daybreak this morning, when arrangements were at once commenced to rescue the man from his perilous situation. The man in the boat was a fisherman, named Johnson. He was on a rock between Goat Island and the Canada shore, and directly above the falls. Notwithstanding the imminent risk, a man named Joel Robinson, at the peril of his life, went to his relief in a small skiff, taking a rope from the island, and succeeded in rescuing him from the boat. About five minutes after Johnson was taken from the boat it loosened from the rock and went over the

WE'LL GIVE HIM ANOTHER
COUPLE OF MINUTES AND
IF HE DOESNT CATCH ANYTHING....

Falls. He had been in that situation since 12 o'clock last night, and was intoxicated. A purse of $200 was made up by the visitors for Robinson.

2 August 1852

PERILOUS ADVENTURE AT NIAGARA FALLS

A correspondent of the Rochester 'Union' writes from Niagara Falls, under date of March 31, as follows:— Mr. Thomas J. Taylor, of West Greenfield, Herkimer county, New York, who had been to Illinois and was on his way home, stopped at this place to wait for a friend whom he expected, and while here he went down the steps at Whitmer's mills, adjoining the bridge, to view the river, and while there sat down upon a large rock and took out his wallet to examine his papers and money, and after a short time he became dizzy and fell into the river. He states that for the first ten rods* he was under the water, and was thrown against large rocks which were under the bridge. When he passed the bridge a gentleman saw him and gave the alarm. He went down the rapids about 200 rods, when he was drawn by the current towards and upon the rocks, to which he clung and got from the water. Our village was aroused in a moment as it were, and the rope ladders belonging to the Bridge Company were brought out and on the spot at once, and let over the bank some 260 feet, when Millard B. Coburn went down and got the ladder over the lower ledge; then a German, name unknown, went down to Taylor, who was almost exhausted with cold. After about half-an-hour Taylor commenced to ascend the ladder. He was some time in getting up. He is a man of about 60 years of age. He was greeted upon his arrival on the bank by a general shout of welcome, and was taken to the La Den House, where, by the kindness of the worthy host, John N. La Den, he was provided with a change of clothing. He is now smart and well, but says it was rather

* A "rod" is the same as a "perch", i.e. 5½ yards.

125

a hard road to travel, and would rather be excused from a second trip. We have named the rock upon which he got out "Taylor's Rock", as he was the first man who ever went there by that route.

21 April 1857

SINGULAR EFFECTS OF AN ACCIDENT ON MONT-BLANC

The 'Medical Times and Gazette' contains the following:— "A party ascending Mont Blanc, consisting of Messrs. H., B., and others, all first-rate mountaineers, with their guides, had slept out all night, and after breakfast Mr. B. left the others for a few minutes, being on a slight slope near a precipice. In returning to the party Mr. B. slipped, fell on his back, and then over. He slid down 1,500 feet at an angle of 45 deg. by measurement, at a velocity of not less than 60 miles an hour, over frozen snow covered by little peas of ice like hail, and was brought up at a crevasse by the collected snow in his clothes; this was owing to the arrangement of his dress at the time of the accident, his trousers, down, had no doubt saved him by tying his legs together. . .

10 August 1861

SAVED BY CRINOLINE

One day last week a lady, named Williamson, belonging to Coventry, was rambling with some friends among the ruins of Kenilworth Castle when she fell over a precipice into the gardens adjacent to the highest accessible portion of the ruins, from a height of about 50 feet. As she descended, her dress, which was extended by crinoline, caught in the ivy which grows so luxuriantly upon the walls of Kenilworth,

thereby breaking to a great extent the force of the collision, and being taken up she was found to have sustained but little external injury. She was of course much bruised and shaken, and it will be some time before she recovers from the severe shock she has received.

28 August 1862

EXTRAORDINARY ACCIDENT

The driver of the mail cart between Horncastle and Langworth was proceeding on his usual journey about half-past 6 o'clock on the evening of the 16th inst. As he entered Wragby one of the traces gave way, and this caused the horse to take fright; the animal rushed off at a furious rate, and the driver lost all control over it. At the corner where the roads diverge, the one leading to Langworth, the other to Market-Rasen, the horse was accustomed to turn up the latter road where the post-office is. As the angle is a sharp one, and the horse was at full speed, he could not manage to turn the corner. Just opposite to him was the house of Mr. Weightman, and in a room on the ground floor the family, with a few friends, in all ten persons, were quietly sitting round the tea table. Into one of the windows of this small room the horse suddenly leaped, carrying with it its harness, and leaving outside the body of the mail cart, with the terror stricken driver sitting in it unhurt. The consternation of the party in the room may be imagined. The horse lighted on a chair which had just been vacated by the tea-maker, he then leapt on the table, breaking into shivers the table, cups and saucers, and all its contents. Terrified by the exploit it had performed,the horse then began kicking and plunging about the room, smashed a chiffonier containing wine and brandy bottles and glasses, broke in pieces a sewing-machine, the chairs and sofa, and nearly all the furniture in the room. For about five or six minutes this work of destruction went on. Some of Mr. Weightman's men came to the door, but at first

128

dared not enter the room to secure the infuriated animal. At last the horse was seized by Mr. Weightman's son, who held him till he was quieted. But he could not return as he entered, so he was led through the kitchen into the back yard, uninjured, except to the extent of a few scratches. The strangest part of the story is the providential escape of all the party unhurt; it seems almost miraculous that not one of them was seriously injured. The youngest, a child aged four, lay at one time under the horse's legs, and another, a few years older, was kicked under the grate, but was not much hurt.

29 March 1867

TRESPASSER ON A RAILWAY

An Indian paper, the 'Pioneer', of October the 23d, says:—
"One day last week a jemadar of pointsmen at Sutna Station

was going along by the side of the rails to let a down train out of the station, when he was seen to stagger wildly about for a few moments, and then fall down close to the rails just as the train was coming on. As soon as the train had passed he was seen lying quite still in the same place, and everyone of course supposed he had been killed by a blow from some part of the engine. Two or three men accordingly came running up, but found the jemadar alive, prostrate on the ballast, with an enormous cobra twined about his legs. Fortunately one of the men had a stick, and began hitting at the cobra with all his might, regardless of the bare shirt of the poor jemadar. The snake was finally killed, and then the jemadar picked himself up, rather ruefully, and explained the whole affair. It appeared that in getting out of the way of the train he trod on the snake, and in trying to dodge the snake he tripped over the wire that works the distant signal, and rolled back towards the train in company with the venomous reptile. The latter was probably frightened at the train, and writhed about the man's legs for protection; the man himself lay as still and flat as possible, and had the satisfaction of seeing the projecting part of the cow-catcher pass about an inch above his nose. His feelings may be better imagined than described when he found himself saved from both perils, uncrushed and unbitten, and none the worse for the adventure, saving for the fright and a hearty belabouring about the legs with a stout bamboo. The above may be relied on."

24 November 1871

TWO NARROW ESCAPES

On June 1 a painter, named M'Cullough, employed at Niagara Falls in painting the bridge which crosses the rapids to the islands known as the Three Sisters, fell into the torrent and was instantly swept away. When destruction seemed inevitable he caught upon a rock hardly fifty feet from the brink of the cataract, and there hung. It seemed as if this could only be a respite. He managed to retain his hold, but the water was exceedingly cold, and it was feared that his limbs would become benumbed and he would be swept away. Happily, however, a man was found bold enough to attempt a rescue and skilful enough to accomplish it. Thomas Conroy, a guide at the Cave of the Winds, fastened a rope round his waist, and, swimming down with the current, succeeded in reaching the imperilled and nearly exhausted painter and drawing him safely to shore in a very exhausted state. The other incident is quite as dramatic and terrible. Patrick M'Arthur, a labouring man, making his way to Detroit in search of work, was walking along the railway track, as the more convenient road, when his foot caught in the "frog" of a switch so tightly that all his efforts failed to extricate it. It was a lonely spot, and his cries for assistance were unheard; the night had fallen, so that his position was unlikely to be detected, and his leg, wrenched by his violent efforts to release himself, grew so painful that he could hardly move it. In this situation he heard the whistle of an approaching train. He had only his own wits to depend on, and these fortunately, did not fail him. He had matches in his pocket, paper and linen in his bundle, and with these he made a sort of torch, which he tied to his walking stick, and, when the train drew near enough, set it on fire. It was a dreadful risk. If he lit his beacon too soon, the wind might blow it out before the engineer had seen it. If he delayed too long, the train might be upon him before the blaze had become visible. Fate befriended him, however, at the last. His signal was seen in time, the train stopped, and, more dead than alive, he was released from his extraordinary prison.

19 June 1874

A PERILOUS POSITION

Our Geneva Correspondent writes:— "A few days since two schoolmasters from Morzine, a Savoyard village near the

Swiss frontier, made an excursion to the Col de Coux, not far from Champéry, in the Valais. As they were descending the mountain, late in the afternoon, they thought they heard cries of distress. After a long search they perceived a man holding on to a bush, or small tree, which had struck its roots into the face of the precipice. As the precipice was nearly perpendicular and the man was some 1,200 ft. below them, and the foot of the precipice quite as far below him, they found it impossible to give the poor fellow any help. All they could do was to tell him to stay where he was – if he could – until they came back, and hurry off to Morzine for help. Though it was night when they arrived thither, a dozen bold mountaineers, equipped with ropes, started forthwith for the rescue. After a walk of 12 miles they reached the Col de la Golèse, but it being impossible to scale the rocks in the dark they remained there until the sun rose. As soon as there was sufficient light they climbed by a roundabout path to the top of the precipice. The man was still holding on to the bush. Three of the rescue party, fastened together with cords, were then lowered to a ledge about 600 feet below. From this coign of vantage two of the three lowered the third to the bush. He found the man, who had been seated astride his precarious perch a day and a night, between life and death. It was a wonder how he had been able to hold on so long, for besides suffering from hunger and cold he had been hurt in the fall from the height above. He was a reserve man belonging to Saméons, on his way thither from Lausanne, where he had been working, to be present at a muster. Losing his way on the mountains between Thonon and Saméons, he had missed his footing and rolled over the precipice. He had the presence of mind to cling to the bush, which broke his fall, but if the two schoolmasters had not heard his cries he must have perished miserably. Hoisting him to the top of the precipice was a difficult and perilous undertaking, but it was safely accomplished. None of the man's hurts were dangerous, and after a long rest and a hearty meal or two he was pronounced fit to continue his journey and report himself at the muster.

12 July 1882

132

NARROW ESCAPE OF THE
COMMANDER OF AN INDIAN ARMY

Major the Nawab Afsur Jung, the commander of the principal brigade of the Nizam's army, had a narrow escape three weeks ago of losing his life by being trampled on by an elephant. The Nawab pitched his tent during the recent Mohurram procession close to the Nizam's palace. One night, just before his Highness was starting for his ride round the city, one of the elephants charged another and smaller one and knocked it over. The smaller elephant fell on the tent at the time when the Nawab was inside. Luckily the elephant did not fall upon him, and the Nawab just managed to escape by crawling from under the wreck of the tent, the bed, washing-stand, &c., being completely smashed.

9 October 1890

General index

Index of places

Africa: Algiers 101; Nyassa 100; Oran 65; Sebluanie river 72; West Cape Colony 25
Belgium: Bruges 87
Canada: 96; Niagara Falls 123, 125, 130; Quebec 31
England: Barnsley 71; Beeston, Notts. 65; Belvoir Hunt 76; Bishopsthorpe, Yorks. 57; Bognor 89; Bolton 80; Bonsall, Derbys. 115; Bootle 77; Borstal, Kent 19; Bradford 81; Brampton, Cumberland 42; Brill, Bucks. 114; Bristol 12, 115; Chard, Somerset 91; Cobham 78; Colchester 6; Clifton, Bristol 115; Crockernwell 3; Doncaster 110; East Leys 114; Exeter 3; Falmouth 3; Glenfield, Leics. 63; Great Horton, Yorks. 34; Halifax 70; Hempstead, Gloucs. 89; Hertford 6; Ipswich 7; Kenilworth Castle 126; Lewes 94; Liscard, Cheshire 39;
  London: 61, 66; Agricultural-hall 18; the American Exhibition 26; Bethnal Green 81; Brixton 37; Brompton Church 52; Coronation of William IV 52; Euston Square 113; Golden Square 34; Hackney 48; House of Lords 58; Lambeth 8, 113; Law Courts 84; Limehouse 90; Lower Grosvenor Street 1, 31; Mile End 83; Oxford Street 45; Ratcliff Highway 13; Sanger's Royal Amphitheatre 21; St. Paul's Cathedral 80; Strand 3; Walworth 77; West India Dock 5; Westminster 102; Whitechapel 86;
Maidstone 107; Maldon, Essex 43; Malpas, Cheshire 81; Mansfield 45; Monk Bretton, Yorks. 69; Newcastle-upon-Tyne 119; Newmarket 20; Norwich 16; Nottingham 15, 67, 103; Penzance 108; Plymouth 36, Portland, Dorset 9; Portsea, Hants. 56; Retford 20; Rossington, Yorks. 26; Rugby 117; Salford 61, 79; Stamford 102; Sturminster, Dorset 32; Thorpe, Lincs. 54; Tranmere 46; Trowbridge 54; Truro 44; Tynemouth 106; Wragby, Lincs. 128
France: Cannes 9; Col de la Golèse 131; Lyons 40; Mont-Blanc 126; Montrouge 98; Nevers 4;
  Paris: 41; Hippodrome 65; Place de la Bastille 91; Rue de Bièvre 30; Rue St. Lazare 120;
Passy 73; Saint Come 4; Versailles 86
Germany: Augsburgh 7; Rhode 24
India: 133; Fyzabad 28; Goodaloor 40; Sutna 129
Ireland: Armagh 16, 111; Dublin 28, 108; Kildare 50; Kilkenny 71
Russia: Peterhoff 49
Scotland: Alloa 93; Dalbeattie 36; Dundee 106; Greenock 44; Kilmarnock 75
Spain: Madrid 25
Switzerland: Berne 70; Mount Pilatus 25; Polmengo Tunnel 50; Soleure 103
U.S.A.: 47; California, Gulf of 11; Cincinnati 50; Detroit 131; Kingston, Rhode Island 87; Middletown, Missouri 96; Ohio 94; Sand-hill, Kentucky 47
Wales: Abergavenny 6; Llangafelach 63; Monmouth 119; Newport, Mon. 121; Swansea 85

136